Strategic Sustainable Procurement

An Overview of Law and Best Practice for the Public and Private Sectors

T0298904

Colleen Theron
Solicitor and Founder and Director of CLT envirolaw

Malcolm Dowden
Solicitor and Director of Law Programmes, Law2020

First published in 2014 by Dō Sustainability

87 Lonsdale Road, Oxford OX2 7ET, UK

ISBN 978-1-910174-25-8 (eBook-ePub)
ISBN 978-1-910174-26-5 (eBook-PDF)
ISBN 978-1-910174-24-1 (Paperback)

A catalogue record for this title is available from the British Library.

Dō Sustainability strives for net positive social and environmental impact. See our sustainability policy at **www.dosustainability.com**.

Page design and typesetting by Alison Rayner
Cover by Becky Chilcott

For further information on Dō Sustainability, visit our website:
www.dosustainability.com

DōShorts

Dō Sustainability is the publisher of DōShorts: short, high-value ebooks that distil sustainability best practice and business insights for busy, results-driven professionals. Each DōShort can be read in 90 minutes.

New and forthcoming DōShorts – stay up to date

We publish 3 to 5 new DōShorts each month. The best way to keep up to date? Sign up to our short, monthly newsletter. Go to **www.dosustainability.com/newsletter** to sign up to the Dō Newsletter. Some of our latest and forthcoming titles include:

- *Building a Sustainable Supply Chain* Gareth Kane
- *Management Systems for Sustainability: How to Successfully Connect Strategy and Action* Phil Cumming
- *Understanding Integrated Reporting: The Concise Guide to Integrated Thinking and the Future of Corporate Reporting* Carol Adams
- *Corporate Sustainability in India: A Practical Guide for Multinationals* Caroline Twigg
- *Networks for Sustainability: Harnessing People Power to Deliver Your Goals* Sarah Holloway
- *Making Sustainability Matter: How To Make Materiality Drive Profit, Strategy and Communications* Dwayne Baraka
- *Creating a Sustainable Brand: A Guide to Growing the Sustainability Top Line* Henk Campher
- *Cultivating System Change: A Practitioner's Companion* Anna Birney

- *How Much Energy Does Your Building Use* Liz Reason
- *Lobbying for Good: How Business Advocacy Can Accelerate the Delivery of a Sustainable Economy* Paul Monaghan & Philip Monaghan
- *Creating Employee Champions: How to Drive Business Success Through Sustainability Engagement Training* Joanna M. Sullivan
- *Smart Engagement: Why, What, Who and How* John Aston & Alan Knight
- *How to Produce a Sustainability Report* Kye Gbangbola & Nicole Lawler

Subscriptions

In addition to individual sales of our ebooks, we now offer subscriptions. Access 60+ ebooks for the price of 5 with a personal subscription to our full e-library. Institutional subscriptions are also available for your staff or students. Visit **www.dosustainability.com/books/subscriptions** or email **veruschka@dosustainability.com**

Write for us, or suggest a DōShort

Please visit **www.dosustainability.com** for our full publishing programme. If you don't find what you need, write for us! Or suggest a DōShort on our website. We look forward to hearing from you.

Abstract

THE STRATEGIC ROLE OF PURCHASING AND SUPPLYING as a lever for sustainable development and corporate social and environmental responsibility is increasingly important. It is manifested in greater regulation on sustainable procurement in the public sector, including significant changes to the EU Directives in April 2014. There is also increased emphasis on 'clean' supply chains in the private sector, as best practice seeks to mesh with public sector requirements and reduce the risk that bids for public contracts might be undermined by adverse environmental impacts or social misconduct along the supply chain. Private sector companies are also increasingly seeking to establish best practice sustainable procurement principles to minimise the risk of litigation. Several international standards are embedding the principles of sustainable procurement into their requirements as well. In both the public and the private sector there are moves to improve the environmental and social performance of companies through supply chain management. In addition, there are instances where private sector organisations need to understand and adopt public sector procurement principles and procedures. Why? Quite simply because many large private sector organisations are seeking access to the estimated €1000 billion a year worldwide trade flows from public procurement, and those private sector bidders must ensure that they, and their supply chains, meet the requirements set by contracting authorities which are, in turn, driven by the need to comply with procurement law, regulation and policy objectives.

....

About the Authors

COLLEEN THERON is tri-qualified as a solicitor in England, Wales, Scotland and South Africa, and holds an LLM in environmental law from the University of Aberdeen (with distinction). Since 1996 she has advised on environmental issues in complex property and corporate transactions, including public sector and MoD matters, in her career as an environmental lawyer in the City of London. The Legal 500 and Chambers recognise Colleen as a leading environmental law practitioner. Colleen retains a role as consultant to law firms and lectures on environmental and sustainability law at Birkbeck University, London.

Colleen is also the founder and director of CLT envirolaw, a niche sustainability company providing specialist advice to companies and directors on sustainability issues. She has specialist knowledge of the event sector, having been a member of the BSI London mirror committee, developing ISO 20121, an international standard for sustainable events. She advises clients on how to develop sustainable procurement policies and implement technical sustainable procurement provisions into tenders and contracts, including implementing policies and procedures on business and human rights.

Colleen is a frequent contributor to the legal and professional press. Some of her publications are available at www.clt-envirolaw.com/publications. She also contributes to *LexisPSL Environment*, providing specialist environmental knowhow on sustainability and responsible business issues. She is the co-author (with Malcolm Dowden) of the UK chapter in the UNEP-funded book *Green Buildings and the Law* (CIB, 2011)

Colleen is passionate about stopping human trafficking and has recently been appointed a director of the NGO Finance against Human Trafficking. She was an executive member and trustee of the UK Environmental Law Association for seven years. She is also part of the newly formed steering group of the British Association for Sustainability in Sport (BASIS). Colleen has had an interest in CSR, corporate reporting and sustainability issues throughout her career and is also a speaker on these issues.

 **MALCOLM DOWDEN** is a solicitor, combining practical legal work as consultant to City of London law firm Charles Russell LLP with his role as Director of Law Programmes with the rapidly growing international legal training business Law2020.

Qualified in 1994, Malcolm has extensive experience of procurement, commercial and real estate transactions, environmental law and regulatory compliance. His work for Charles Russell LLP has also included regulatory and legislative drafting for a Commonwealth government.

As well as advising clients on public and private sector procurement matters, including legal challenge to procurement procedures and decisions, Malcolm has designed and delivered practical training courses for local authorities in the UK and has also presented conference papers and training courses on procurement in a range of other jurisdictions, most recently, India. Through Law2020 Malcolm is accredited by the

Solicitors Regulation Authority to provide professional training. He has also delivered master class sessions for Asian Legal Business, accredited by the Singapore Institute of Legal Education.

Malcolm is a frequent contributor to the legal and professional press, including the *Estates Gazette* and *New Law Journal*. He is the author of *Climate Change and Sustainable Development* (EG Books, 2008) and co-author (with Colleen Theron) of the UK chapter in the UNEP-funded book *Green Buildings and the Law* (CIB, 2011)

....

Disclaimer

THIS BOOK IS INTENDED TO PROVIDE an introduction to and comprehensive summary of sustainable procurement, for both the public and
private sectors, but does not reflect the entire breadth of the subject
in detail. It provides some examples of case studies and drafting as a
snapshot to help practitioners understand how to apply the principles of
procuring sustainably.

Who Is This Book For?

THIS BOOK IS AIMED AT A WIDE RANGE OF PROFESSIONALS and other stakeholders who have a professional, personal or academic interest in sustainable procurement. The table below offers some guidance on who this book might be relevant for and why.

WHO?	WHY?
Procurement professionals or any employee with purchasing responsibility in large companies.	This book distils key developments in public procurement legislation and sustainable procurement more broadly. It provides an introduction to and practical examples of what strategic sustainable procurement entails, whether the organisation is bidding for public sector contracts, in need of meeting tender requirements, looking to obtain certification for a standard, or is simply seeking to improve its supply chain management and implement best practice.

WHO?	WHY?
A Chief Procurement Officer (CPO) seeking to understand the latest in sustainable procurement and how it might fit within the broader procurement strategy.	A CPO charged with the strategic direction of procurement will have to stay on top what is up and coming and have an understanding of growing importance of sustainability considerations in procurement. This book provides a succinct account of the barriers, drivers, costs and gains involved in embedding sustainable procurement and offers some practical starting points for implementation.
An SME owner or manager.	Under new legislation and latest government policy there will be increased opportunities for SMEs to win public sector contracts. Whether seeking to compete for public sector contracts, or simply wanting to manage supply chain risks and move towards best practice, this book provides an accessible overview of sustainable procurement as it stands and where it is headed – from the background to some practical starting points.
Personnel from a public sector authority or department (e.g. local council) or any other organisation who is involved in setting out requirements for tenders.	Civil servants enlisted to set out tender requirements will have to make sure they are in accordance with legislation. This book provides an overview of legislation and government guidance and policy and where else to look for further information. Personnel from non-state entities may seek to follow the public sector example when developing their tender requirements.

WHO?	WHY?
A CEO seeking to understand the latest in sustainable procurement and how it might fit within the broader business strategy and the organisation's long-term vision.	Although CEOs are not involved in the detail of procurement decisions or sustainability programmes, this book will provide a high level understanding of key trends and developments in the field of procurement and an introduction into why and how these should be fed into the wider business strategy to generate value for an organisation and align with best practice.
A sustainability consultant supporting strategic sustainability programmes in companies.	The rise of sustainable supply chain management and growing legal requirements around procurement reinforces the need for process and focus on major sustainability issues. By acquiring an understanding of and embedding sustainable procurement considerations into the expertise you offer, your contribution will have more value and greater impact.
Auditors and certifiers.	This book will offer context to the procurement standards that auditors and certifiers work with and provide a succinct update of key trends and developments in sustainable procurement.

What Does This Book Do?

THE AIM OF THIS BOOK will be to:

- define and identify the differences between key concepts: sustainable and ethical procurement

- explain current EU and UK public sustainable procurement legislation, government guidance and policy

- introduce the principal sustainable procurement standards and best practice principles for the private sector

- develop understanding of the drivers and barriers to adopting a sustainable procurement strategy for public and private sector

- outline the basics of a sustainable procurement strategy

- help develop a sustainable procurement policy

- understand how to overcome 'silo' thinking and who should be involved in the process, including an overview of working with suppliers

- provide practical examples of the of sustainable procurement from the selection, award and contract management stages of the procurement process that can be used in public and private sector procurement and that will include:

  - a risk assessment checklist

– an overview of Smart SPP, together with a case study and template

– a discussion on weighting criteria with examples of weighting scorecards

– an explanation of key contractual terms and issues to consider when reviewing contracts

Contents

CHAPTER 1
Introduction

WHY DO PRIVATE SECTOR ORGANISATIONS need to understand and adopt public sector procurement principles and procedures? Quite simply because many large private sector organisations are seeking access to the estimated €1000 billion a year worldwide trade flows from public procurement,[1] and those private sector bidders must ensure that they, and their supply chains, meet the requirements set by contracting authorities which are, in turn, driven by the need to comply with procurement law, regulation and policy objectives.

The strategic role of purchase and supply as a lever for sustainable development and corporate social and environmental responsibility is increasingly important. It is not only manifested in greater regulation on sustainable procurement in the public sector, including significant changes to the EU Directives adopted in April 2014, requiring implementation within two years by EU Member States. There is also increased emphasis on 'clean' supply chains in the private sector, not least to reduce the risk that bids for public contracts might be undermined, or even ruled out that the pre-qualification stage, by adverse environmental impacts or social misconduct along the supply chain. Private sector companies are also increasingly seeking to establish best practice sustainable procurement principles to minimise the risk of litigation. Several international standards are embedding the principles of sustainable procurement into their requirements as well. In both the public and the private sector there are moves to improve the environmental and social performance of companies through supply chain management.

However, sustainability and sustainable development are neither the sole nor even the principal objectives of procurement. Indeed, until relatively recently public sector procurement procedures could not legitimately be used to advance broader social policy objectives such as environmental performance or sustainability unless a clear and objective connection could be made with 'value for money'. The use of public sector purchasing power as a lever for broader policy objectives depends in large measure on the ability to move from evaluation and award criteria geared to the lowest price and towards criteria designed to identify the Most Economically Advantageous Tender (MEAT). The MEAT approach allows procurement professionals to achieve the 'five rights' – the right quantity of the right quality at the right time, from the right source and at the right cost.

Beginning with legislation, international standards and the scope for legal challenge, this book provides direct and actionable guidance to professionals who need to write sustainability specifications, design and implement evaluation and award criteria and manage delivery of contracts, using risk management enhanced by adopting a more sustainable approach. A key issue to be tackled by organisations over the long term will be addressing the relationship between sustainability and value creation.

During a series of preliminary workshop sessions that led to production of this book, we developed and discussed a series of case studies designed to contextualise, explore and test the principles. They are set out below, and referred to throughout the text.

Sustainable Procurement Case Study

The Central Counties Purchasing Organisation (CCPO) is one of the UK's largest public sector professional buying organisations. It operates on a not-for-profit cost recovery basis and is committed to delivering best value to its customers, suppliers and local communities. CCPO is also committed to the promotion and adoption of e-procurement and to embedding the principles of sustainable procurement.

CCPO primarily serves:

- the education sector (schools, academies, colleges and universities)

- local authorities

- central government agencies and ministries

- the NHS and emergency services ('blue light' services)

CCPO is currently working on the following matters, intended to serve as best practice models:

Procurement of energy solutions for local authority housing and education:
The overall brief is to achieve measurable reductions in 1) energy costs, 2) greenhouse gas emissions and 3) energy efficiency ratings. A key challenge for CCPO is to achieve those results across a mixed portfolio of properties. Participating contracting authorities are

also keen to promote local employment and business opportunities and to demonstrate strong sustainability credentials. To that end, CCPO has been instructed so far as possible to consider how far the overall project can be broken down into lot sizes likely to attract bids from small and medium-sized enterprises within the areas served by the contracting authorities. There is also a strong policy directive from the contracting authorities to ensure that the process promotes the development of innovative technologies and techniques.

Procurement of catering services for a major new leisure and conference facility associated with a new arena to be used by a premier league ice hockey team and as training facilities for the national ice skating association's elite skaters:

The venue is to be used for conferences, weddings and other large-scale social events. The ice rink is convertible for use as a concert venue. Freehold ownership of the scheme is to remain with the contracting authority. Catering services are to be procured directly by the contracting authority and sublet to private sector organisations using the facilities, including the national ice skating association. CCPO's remit is to ensure that the catering services meet the highest standards of sustainability, and the contracting authority has made it clear that it is committed to supporting the Fair Trade initiative and to ensuring that any events held at the facility can be certified 'carbon neutral'. They are also wondering if they should adopt ISO20121 as a benchmark.

Procurement of clothing, linen and laundry services for hospitals and 'blue light' services:

CCPO recently commissioned a research report that highlighted the environmental impacts of laundry services for hospitals and 'blue light' services. Based on that report a group of contracting authorities within CCPO's region have commissioned CCPO to develop a procurement approach that would significantly reduce the relevant impacts. CCPO's remit specifically includes an instruction to consider issues such as the sourcing of uniforms, linen and other materials required for the efficient operation of the relevant services.

CHAPTER 2

Defining Key Concepts

What is sustainable procurement?

THE WORKING DEFINITION of sustainable procurement proposed by the Sustainable Procurement Task Force (**https://www.gov.uk/ government/publications/procuring-the-future**) is: 'A process whereby organisations meet their needs for goods, services, works and utilities in a way that achieves value for money on a whole life basis in terms of generating benefits not only to the organisation, but also to society and the economy, whilst minimising damage to the environment.'[2] Sustainable procurement is broader than, and must not be confused with the term Green Public Procurement (GPP),[3] which emphasises only the environmental impact throughout the lifecycle of goods, services or works. Sustainable Procurement isn't simply about being 'green'; it includes social and economic considerations, too.

A joint paper by PWC and Ecovadis[4] ('the PWC report' – **http://saulnier conseil.com/wp-content/uploads/2011/01/Value-of-Sustainable-Suppliers-INSEAD-Dec-2010.pdf**) describes sustainable procurement as 'taking into account economical, environmental and social impacts in buying choices. This includes optimising price, quality and availability, but also environmental life-cycle impact and social aspects linked to product/services origin.'

Environmental life-cycle

The significance of environmental life-cycle impact was highlighted by a project that formed the basis for our case study concerning the procurement of clothing, linen and laundry for hospitals and 'blue light' services. That case study stemmed from an exemplary project conducted by the City of Zurich in 2008–09. The project involved the procurement of workwear, initially for the police force.

http://ec.europa.eu/environment/gpp/pdf/casestudy8.pdf

A pilot was conducted in which 525 100% organic cotton shirts were purchased and presented for user and laboratory tests. On the basis of better performance and user satisfaction, a tender procedure for the annual purchase of approximately 4000 shirts was launched, using the following criteria:

Subject matter of the contract: Procurement of 100% organic cotton police shirts.

Specification: 100% organic cotton, non-iron long and short-sleeved shirts with detailed finishing. Fabric must comply with the Eco-Tex Standard 100 Class II or equivalent. The criteria underlying this standard set limit values for potentially harmful substances at all stages of processing for textiles which are in direct contact with skin. The standard also sets requirements for the use of biologically active and flame-retardant products and minimum levels of colour-fastness.

While the raw material costs for organic cotton are higher than non-organic, the overall effect on the price of the finished garments is minimal – the cost per shirt is approximately 10% higher. However, the higher initial purchase price must be assessed in light of the improved quality and corresponding longer life expectancy of the shirts. 1000 police officers have benefited from these higher-quality and lower-impact garments since 2009.

The production of non-organic cotton is an intensive agricultural process, with the use of pesticides and mineral fertilisers affecting soil and water quality and biodiversity, as well as generating greenhouse gas (GHG) emissions. Further GHG emissions accrue at the spinning, dyeing and finishing stages, as well as during transportation and use of the finished product. Zürich identified a potential difference of 5 kg CO_2e per kilogram of cotton fibre when organic and non-organic production methods were compared. Further reductions were realised by the use of 20% hydropower at the spinning mill and heat recovery at the dye house. While the total volume of GHG emissions saved is relatively low, the cost per tonne of CO_2e reduction compares favourably with other possible measures (such as building improvements), making the purchase of textiles a 'low-hanging fruit' for authorities wishing to implement greener purchasing.

BS8903[5] defines sustainable procurement as 'good procurement and should not be viewed as an abstract, idealistic goal but as a practical and achievable objective for all organisations, large and small'.

The Queensland Government (**www.hpw.qld.gov.au/SiteCollection Documents/SustainableProcurementDefinition.pdf**) defines sustainable procurement as 'a process whereby organisations meet their needs for goods, services and capital projects, in a way that achieves value for money on a whole life basis in terms of generating benefits not only to the organisation, but also to society, the economy and the natural environment'.

All of these definitions highlight the integration of economic, social and environmental issues as part of the consideration in developing a sustainable procurement strategy to deliver value for money.

Are sustainable and ethical procurement the same thing?

According to the CIPS (**www.cips.org/Documents/About%20CIPS/CIPS_Ethics_Guide_WEB.pdf**), ethical procurement can be defined as procurement processes that respect fundamental international standards against criminal conduct, such as bribery, corruption and fraud and human rights abuses, including human trafficking.[6] In companies that apply an integrated approach to managing their risks, ethical procurement requirements will fall under their sustainability framework and within their sustainable procurement strategy.

To address business risk of unethical procurement, many businesses will have established a code of conduct, setting out the minimum standards and parameters for procurement. Codes of conduct refer to an expected way of behaving. They can be supplemented by mainstreaming their ethical values throughout the procurement policy. For example, the procurement policy may include identifying those practices that are unacceptable (such as slavery and fraud) and how the organisation will deal with conduct that violates the organisation's policy and any code of conduct signed up to by the supplier.

Organisations should therefore ensure that principles set out in their codes of conduct are reflected in their procurement strategy and purchasing decisions.

To what extent are ethical considerations relevant to sustainable procurement?

The screening of bids based on ethical considerations is often limited to a requirement for certification that a supplier has not recently violated any laws that prohibit bribery, environmental compliance or employment issues. There is often a gap that under the current requirements where business ethics do not extend to compliance with human rights. In the International Corporate Accountability Roundtable (ICAR) (http:// accountabilityroundtable.org/wp-content/uploads/2014/01/ICAR-Government-Procurement-Project-Geneva-Summary-Document-Final.pdf) summary study on what human rights are applicable to US government procurement, they suggest that this gap should be made more clear and potential or real violations in a tenderer's supply chain should be evaluated.[7]

Nonetheless, the tendency to require ethical considerations in tenders is likely to grow. An example of how a government and governing organisations have had to respond to concerns about the plight of workers is during the building of the 2022 FIFA World Cup football stadiums. Qatar Supreme Committee's Workers' Charter (**www.qf.org. qa/app/media/2379**) was published in early 2014 and requires that any company wanting to bid on the construction of any of the Qatar World Cup construction projects will have to comply with the requirements of the Workers' Charter and demonstrate how they are going to implement its requirements. Key to the ability to submit any tender will be a Workers'

Charter Plan which includes requirements that the bidding company will ensure that they work with accredited recruitment agencies and that working and living conditions meet certain requirements. Whether these requirements are enforced in practice as build up towards the 2022 event continues remains yet to be seen.

Why should companies focus on ethical and sustainable procurement?

This book will consider the drivers for both the public and private sectors to embed sustainable procurement practices. Nonetheless, it is worth highlighting from the outset that companies are increasingly focusing on improving their supply chain management and transparency in order to:

- minimise legal risk (e.g. bribery and corruption)

- minimise operational risk (e.g. strikes; product unavailability)

- prevent reputational damage (e.g. arising from 'sweat shop' labour conditions)

- avoid incurring costs from negative externalities (e.g. pollution clean ups)

The impact of the disaster of the Rana Plaza (**www.bbc.co.uk/news/world-asia-27107860**), the 'Happy eggs' scandal,[8] and the increased media attention given to exploited workers, forced labour and human trafficking is increasing the pressure on organisations, including public authorities, to understand and prioritise dealing with human rights and ethical issues, as well as environmental impacts.[9]

....

CHAPTER 3

The Legislative Position

THERE ARE EU AND UK REGULATIONS that govern the sustainable procurement process by public bodies.

Incoming changes to the law

At the time of writing, those regulations are undergoing a process of significant change. Three new directives came into force on 17 April 2014, marking the start of a two-year period within which EU Members States must implement new rules into national law.

Directive 2014/24 applies to public sector entities and will replace the existing Directive 2004/18/EC (and, as a result, the 2006 Regulations referred to below).

Public sector entities will be obliged to comply with new rules that include:

- abolition of the distinction between Part A and Part B services and its replacement with a more limited set of specialist services (e.g. legal, social and educational services) which will be subject to a 'lighter touch' regulatory regime, requiring OJEU advertisement only if the contract value exceeds a threshold currently set at €750,000.

- express provision for early market engagement or 'pre-commercial' procedures designed to identify possible sources of supply or innovation.

- permission to use a new competitive procedure that allows greater scope for negotiation, for example where a contracting authority's needs cannot be met without adaptation or bespoking of currently available solutions, or where negotiations are justified by reference to the nature, complexity or risk-profile of the contract.

- the ability to exclude bidders from procurement processes on the grounds of poor performance under previous public contracts.

- encouragement of bids from small- and medium-sized enterprises (SMEs), for example by providing that contracting authorities may not set a minimum turnover requirement at more than double the contract value.

- shorter minimum time limits for bidders to respond to notices or submit tenders in order to speed up the procurement process.

- express provision allowing a contracting authority when comparing tenders to take into account the qualifications and experience of individual staff identified for the performance of service contracts. Previously, this ability was limited to initial short-listing and was not available as an award criterion.

- new provisions governing the requirement to go back out to tender where changes occur or are made during the term of an existing contract. For example, re-tender would not be required where a change in contract value falls below the relevant threshold for application of the Directive in respect of new contracts, and the change does not exceed 10% of the initial value of the contract (15% for works contracts).

Directive 2014/25 applies to procurement in the transport, water, energy and postal sectors. The new Directive replaces Directive 2004/17 as implemented by the Utilities Contracts Regulations 2006.

The EU reform package also includes a new Directive 2014/23 on the award of concessions. Concessions are contracts under which a private sector entity obtains the right to charge end-users for the provision of works or services. Familiar examples of works concessions include the construction of a bridge or road where the contractor is given the right to collect and retain tolls paid by users once the infrastructure is in operation. Service concessions include rail franchises and the licence to operate the National Lottery. This new Directive applies to the award of any works or services concession by a public authority where the estimated value exceeds €5 million. Where estimated value exceeds that threshold concessions must be advertised in the *OJEU* and then awarded on the basis of objective and specified criteria.

The UK government response to the new suite of Directives has been positive, so implementation is expected within the two year period allowed to EU Member States. Until implementation, the existing law continues to apply.

The current legal framework in the UK

Public Procurement Regulations 2006 (the '2006 Regulations')[10]

The 2006 Regulations transposed the EU directive 2004/18/EC[11] (http://eur-lex.europa.eu/LexUriServ/LexUriServ.do?uri=CELEX:32004 L0018:en:NOT) on public procurement into the UK. The EU directive:

- aimed to 'clarify, simplify and modernise existing European legislation on public procurement';[12]

- was based on principles of principles of transparency, non-discrimination and competitive procurement;[13]

- sought to ensure that public sector bodies award contracts in an efficient and non-discriminatory manner;[14]

- sought to clarify how contracting authorities '. . . may contribute to the protection of the environment and the promotion of sustainable development, whilst ensuring the possibility of obtaining the best value for money for their contracts'.[15]

- Subject to certain exclusions (e.g. public telecommunications contracts)[16] the 2006 Regulations apply to:

  - a proposed public supply contract,[17]

  - public works contract.[18]

Under the 2006 Regulations there are different rules according to whether the contracts are Part A or Part B contracts.[19] As noted above, that distinction is being abolished under three new directives adopted by the EU in February 2014 and published in the *Official Journal of the EU* on 28 March 2014. The new directives formally entered into force on 17 April 2014 and give EU Member States two years to implement them into national law. Even under the current law the distinction between Part A and Part B services relates only to the extent and formality of the procedures applicable to a particular procurement (for example, whether an *OJEU* advertisement is required). All procurements, even those falling below threshold, must comply with the basic EU procurement principles of:

- non-discrimination

- equal treatment of bidders

- transparency

- proportionality

The rules set out in the 2006 Regulations only apply to a proposed public contract, framework agreement or dynamic purchasing system where the estimated value at the time is less than the relevant threshold (net of value added tax).[20],[21]

These thresholds differ according to whether an entity is a Schedule 1 entity (generally a central government authority) or any other contracting authority.

Further information is available about what must be included in the calculation (see Regulation 8).

Public Services (Social Value) Act 2012

The Public Services (Social Value) Act 2012 (www.gov.uk/government/ uploads/system/uploads/attachment_data/file/275719/Public_ Services__Social_Value__Act_-_One_Year_On.pdf) came into force on 31 January 2013. It requires public sector agencies, when commissioning a public service, to consider how the service they are procuring could bring added economic, environmental and social benefits. Contracting authorities also have to consider whether they should consult on these issues (for instance with potential users or suppliers of the service in question).

The Act is one of a number of pieces of legislation and guidance which together set a clear framework for considering social value in commissioning. For instance:

The Cabinet Office's lean standard operating process places a heavy emphasis on engagement with supply markets before procurement processes commence, and the requirements of the Social Value Act complement this approach.

The Compact, an agreement between the Government (and its associated Non Departmental Public Bodies, Arm's Length Bodies and Executive Agencies) and civil society organisations in England, commits the Government to ensuring that social, environmental and economic value forms a standard part of designing, developing and delivering services.

Various regulations and guidance for particular groups of commissioners also complement the Social Value Act. For instance, a number of agencies under the Duty of Best Value (such as local authorities, police forces, fire authorities and commissioners of transport services) are required to consider the overall value contributed by providers, with the aim of encouraging greater voluntary, community and social enterprise (VCSE) and small and medium enterprise (SME) participation in public services. This duty includes considering the wider economic, environmental and social value created through procurement, above and beyond that of the service itself. Social value and sustainable procurement are also embedded in the NHS Standards of Procurement, as well as forthcoming NHS England Procurement Guidance. The Act builds on these frameworks, extending social value requirements to all contracting bodies and providing clear legal grounds for commissioners to achieve wider impact through procurement.

Procurement Reform (Scotland) Act 2014

The Act imposes a general sustainable procurement duty on contracting authorities in Scotland. It requires high spending contracting authorities to publish a procurement strategy and annual report and requires all contracting authorities to:

- consider imposing 'community benefit requirements' in relation to contracts with a value of £4 million or more; and

- publish notices on a new Public Contracts website[22]

Private sector regulation

There is currently no legislation that *directly* mandates sustainable procurement for the private sector. However, where a private sector organisation wants to tender for public contracts, pre-qualification, evaluation and award criteria commonly require private sector bidders to demonstrate environmental and broader sustainability credentials both in relation to their own organisation and for key elements of their supply chain.

In the private sector, many organisations are adopting the principles of public procurement to ensure that social and environmental issues are taken into account in the tenders and subsequent contracts and to minimise the risk of litigation. Litigation, for example, may be based on misrepresentation stemming from information given in the procurement process in relation to companies forming part of the bidder's supply chain. Misrepresentation, whether innocent, negligent or fraudulent, might result in the loss of a contract, rescinded on the basis of a repudiatory breach. Damages may be payable in addition to or instead of repudiation. Crucially, if a misrepresentation is found to be fraudulent, then any contractual cap on liability might be irrelevant. In a leading private sector procurement case, fraudulent misrepresentation as to the bidder's capacity to deliver an IT project on time led to a claim for £700 million. This greatly exceeded the contractual liability cap of £30 million and also the contract value of £48 million. The claim eventually settled for a reported £318 million.[23]

It is also an increasing trend that buyers are asking suppliers to provide environmental and social initiatives. In some cases, suppliers are gaining business by using environmental initiatives and objectives particularly using innovation, for example, in relation to waste reduction, GHG reduction and energy reduction.[24]

EU and UK guidance and policy on sustainable procurement

Both the EU and the UK have published guidance on sustainable procurement.

UK guidance

The UK government provides guidance on the DEFRA Sustainable Procurement website (**http://sd.defra.gov.uk/advice/public/buying/ background/**). This includes:

- National Sustainable Public Procurement Programme (**www.gov.uk/ government/publications/procuring-the-future**): a training course on sustainable procurement for contracting authorities and a prioritisation tool

- other guidance on sustainable timber procurement (**www.cpet.org.uk**)

- a framework tool for measuring progress (**http://webarchive. nationalarchives.gov.uk/20140827110041/http://sd.defra.gov. uk/advice/public/tools/**)

- guidance from the Olympics with case studies

- Greening Government Commitments (www.gov.uk/government/
  uploads/system/uploads/attachment_data/file/61172/Greening
  _20Government_20Commitments_20-_20guidance_20on_20
  measurement_20and_20reporting.pdf) reporting guidance that
  includes a chapter on sustainable procurement

EU guidance

The EU provides a range guidance and communications on its dedicated
GPP website including guidance relating to:

- life-cycle costing, including an explanation of how it works.[25]

- using public procurement to promote environmental improvement.[26]

- including social considerations (e.g. local employment opportunities and economic benefits) in public procurement.

- integrating environmental considerations into public procurement.[27]

- using pre-commercial procurement (market research and early engagement with potential suppliers) to ensure sustainable high quality public services in Europe.

- the role of Fair Trade and non-governmental trade-related sustainability assurance schemes.[28]

- Buying Green (http://ec.europa.eu/environment/gpp/buying_handbook_en.htm).[29]

Buying Green

The EU handbook (http://ec.europa.eu/environment/gpp/pdf/hand
book.pdf), produced in conjunction with ICLEI[30] sets out approaches and

ideas for 'greening' contracts. ICLEI is a global association of cities and local governments with membership including 12 mega-cities, 100 super-cities and urban regions, 450 large cities and 450 small and medium-sized cities and towns in 84 countries. It was founded in 1990 as 'International Council for Local Environmental Initiatives', but is now formally known by its initials, ICLEI. Although this book deals with sustainable procurement and develops a holistic approach to procurement strategy and policy, where a product or a service has a distinct environmental aspect, these guidelines will be useful in identifying the environmental criteria. The EU GPP criteria cover 18 product and service groups and are available in both core and comprehensive versions.

Examples of green contracts[31]

- energy efficient computers

- low energy buildings

- recycled paper

- cleaning services using environmentally friendly products

- electric, hybrid or low-emission vehicles

CHAPTER 4

Sustainable Procurement Policy in the EU and UK

UK policy

IN 2011, THE UK GOVERNMENT set out its Greening Government commitments with an intended outcome for 2014/15 to procure more sustainably and reduce supply chain impacts. The Defra 'Action Plan for driving sustainable operations and procurement across government' (**http://archive.defra.gov.uk/sustainable/government/documents/ap-driving-sustain-ops.pdf**) discussed these commitments. [32] It included the following key milestones:

- improve and publish data on supply chain impacts, and

- embed Government Buying Standards (GBS) (**www.gov.uk/government/policies/making-sustainable-development-a-part-of-all-government-policy-and-operations**) (i.e. product specifications that provide minimum and best practice levels in 11 product areas) in procurement.[33]

The central government departments and their related organisations must ensure that they meet minimum mandatory specifications in the GBS when buying products and services.

EU policy

Europe 2020 Strategy: A European strategy for smart, sustainable and inclusive growth identifies procurement as part of its 'Roadmap to a Resource Efficient Europe'. It identifies GPP as a demand-led initiative that will be promoted and will need to be implemented by Member States.

The EU has set out its 'Sustainable Consumption and Production and Sustainable Industrial Policy (SCP/SIP) Action Plan' (**http://ec.europa.eu/environment/eussd/escp_en.htm**) to improve the energy and environmental performance of products and foster their uptake by consumers. As part of this the EU plans to strengthen GPP through voluntary measures such as:

- the setting of indicative targets based on the level of best performing Member States

- providing model tender specifications, which are in line with Internal Market legislation, and

- the creation of a process of co-operation with the Member States to identify and agree upon common GPP criteria for products and services for endorsement in national action plans and guidance on GPP.

CHAPTER 5

Sustainable Procurement: The Role of Standards

THE NATURE, SCOPE AND SPEED of economic changes have presented new strategic challenges for organisations and their stakeholders. There is greater demand that companies disclose information on issues that are material to their operations. There are also an increasing number of national and international standards that aim to encourage organisations (including consumers) to make more sustainable production and purchasing choices.[34] Standards are often adopted by both public and private sector organisations to specify performance requirements or as a means of achieving best practice.

Referring to international standards can be a highly effective way to ensure that works, goods or services meet quality assurance or other relevant criteria. Standards may determine whether technological equipment is compatible with equipment that is already in place (for example, electronic communications apparatus) or that it meets specified benchmarks for sustainability. For example, UK Central Government departments, Executive Agencies and Non-Departmental public bodies must adhere to the UK procurement policy on timber, which requires that all timber and wood-derived products must be from independently verifiable legal and sustainable sources.

Once awarded, the contract should include clauses requiring the contractor to provide evidence that any products delivered comply with the policy. However, any such contract clauses will come into operation only once the contract has been awarded. Consequently, when producing specifications it is advisable either to include those requirements in the description of the works, goods or services to be provided or to annex the proposed form of contract including those clauses as part of the tender pack.

There are legal risks to consider when specifying by reference to standards. Within the EU a core function of procurement law is to support and facilitate the free movement of goods, services, capital and persons. Consequently, writing a specification by reference solely to a British Standard may risk challenge where there is an equivalent or similar standard in one or more other EU Member States. For that reason, standards should be employed in the following order:

- International/European Standards

- British Standards

- Industry or company standards

Similar concerns apply to other certification or labelling schemes. A particular scheme (e.g. the German-initiated Blue Angel Standard) might be a credible and independently awarded designation, but it is not the only label potentially applicable to the protection goals that it addresses: health, climate, water and resources. However, conformity with Blue Angel Standards is verified by a third party following an international standard, ISO 17011. Consequently, if a procurement specification were to require that any labelling or accreditation covering water protection or stewardship met those ISO verification standards then Blue Angel labelling could legitimately be taken into account, along with other schemes meeting the same criteria. By contrast, if a procurement specification were to require Blue Angel accreditation then it would exclude other, potentially comparable, schemes and may be open to legal challenge.

Government buying standards

The UK Government has designed Government Buying Standards to simplify sustainable procurement.[35]

They are set at two levels:

- mandatory standards – where all central government depart-ments and their related organisations must ensure they meet the mandatory Government Buying Standards when buying goods and services for those product groups covered.

- best practice – for organisations that want to take a lead in sustainability can choose to find products that meet best practice standards.

There are currently 10 standards,[36] covering construction, construction products, cleaning products and services, electrical goods, food and catering services, furniture, horticulture and park services, office ICT equipment, paper and paper products, textiles, transport and water using products and wood products.

The Standards set out the mandatory and best practice information for each area. For example, if a government organisation or other organisation is buying wood, the standard would look like this:

....

WOOD PRODUCTS STANDARDS V2.0[37]

IMPACT AREA	MANDATORY
Timber	Timber must be purchased in accordance with UK timber procurement policy. Only timber and timber products originating either from independently verified legal and sustainable sources or from a licensed Forest Law Enforcement Governance and Trade (FLEGT) partner can be purchased. Recycled timber is also accepted (TPAN April 2010 for further detail).

IMPACT AREA	BEST PRACTICE
Timber	Same as mandatory standard

A specification is also provided and is set out below:

IMPACT AREA	MANDATORY
Timber	Timber must be purchased in accordance with UK timber procurement policy
	Only timber and timber products originating either from independently verified legal and sustainable sources or from a licensed Forest Law Enforcement Governance and Trade (FLEGT) partner can be purchased Enforcement Governance and Trade (FLEGT) partner can be purchased

IMPACT AREA	BEST PRACTICE
Timber	Same as mandatory standard

BS8903: Principles and Framework for Procurement

BS8903 (http://shop.bsigroup.com/ProductDetail/?pid=0000000000 30203003) is the world's first standard on sustainable procurement. It was published in September 2010.[38] It builds on current best practice and provides guidance on adopting and embedding sustainable procurement principles across all stages of the procurement process.

BS8903 adopts a generic approach to sustainable procurement, building on a flexible framework. It sets out the reasons to procure sustainably and provides an overview of a typical procurement process, identifying the sustainability considerations and activities that ought to be addressed across various points in the process.

The principles set out in the standard apply to both public and private sector organisations. It advises that proper legal advice is always sought, particularly for public procurement requirements that must be read in conjunction with the latest Directives, Regulations and government policy.

ISO20121

ISO20121 (http://www.iso.org/iso/iso20121) is an international standard that specifies the requirements of an event sustainability management system to improve the sustainability of events. Although it follows the 'Plan, Do, Check, Act' formula of other international standards, it is focused more on the strategic aspects of the organisation and is therefore not simply a 'tick box' exercise.

A key element of the standard is supply chain management.

The organisation is required to establish the relevance of its sustainability objectives, targets and plans to individual suppliers. The standard requires that sufficient and relevant information is provided in tenders and other documentation to enable its suppliers to demonstrate their capability to support their objectives.

The standard requires that organisations will make assessments of tenders or equivalent documents based on the supplier's ability to meet or contribute towards objectives, targets, cost-effectiveness and quality.

Where organisations do not go through a tender process they are to explain and justify their process and show how they consider sustainable development issues when choosing their suppliers.

Practical guidance is also provided in the standard to help organisations understand how to manage sustainability in their procurement. It emphasises the requirement to engage with a wide range of suppliers and to integrate sustainable development issues into all aspects of the procurement cycle. These aspects are dealt with in more detail later in this book.

ISO 20121 suggests that four key aims are addressed when integrating sustainable development management into the procurement process. These are:

a. minimising negative impacts of products and or services (e.g. impacts on health, quality, generation of hazardous waste)

b. minimising demand for resources

c. minimising negative impacts of the supply chain itself, in particular social aspects (e.g. giving preference to local suppliers) and to meet the minimum ethical, human rights and employment standards

d. ensuring that fair contract terms are applied and respected.

There is also an emphasis in considering sustainable development issues at the earliest stage of the procurement process by building criteria into the product or service specifications.

Case Study

Procurement of catering services for a major new leisure and conference facility associated with a new arena to be used by a premier league ice hockey team and as training facilities for the national ice skating association's elite skaters:

The venue is to be used for conferences, weddings and other large-scale social events. The ice rink is convertible for use as a concert venue. Freehold ownership of the scheme is to remain with the contracting authority. Catering services are to be procured directly by the contracting authority and sublet to private sector organisations using the facilities, including the national ice skating association. CCPO's remit is to ensure that the catering services meet the highest standards of sustainability, and the contracting authority has made it clear that it is committed to supporting the Fair Trade initiative and to ensuring that any events held at the facility can be certified 'carbon neutral'. They are also wondering if they should adopt ISO20121 as a benchmark.

In this case study, we assumed that the contracting authority would be looking to develop a sustainability management system either under ISO20121 or on a basis that is compatible with that

---

standard. As such the organisation has to consider how it is going to reflect the sustainability requirements into the catering tender and contracts. An example of the type of requirement they may include in the pre-qualification[39] and tender documents are:[40]

- a programme or system in place to identify environmental impacts relevant to the organisation/or a programme/system under development with a timeline for implementation[41]

- a copy of a company's sustainable procurement policy

The project involves from the outset the procurement of catering services on the basis that they will be sublet to the private sector sports organisations that will be using the facility. Given the high profile of the sports organisations, both at club and national level, it is highly likely that their requirements will be informed by environmental and sustainability criteria. Large and high profile sports organisations are highly likely to be subject to intense scrutiny from media and NGOs seeking to highlight examples of 'greenwashing' or inflated claims to sustainability criteria. The context would therefore allow (indeed it may require) the contracting authority at least to take account of any specific sustainability and other relevant criteria adopted by those organisations.

The contracts providing for use of the facility by the sports organisations would be highly likely to include specific obligations and warranties on the part of the contracting authority in respect of environmental performance and sustainability criteria. The contract for catering services would be a crucial component in the contracting authority's performance of its own obligations and in compliance with its warranties.

Fair trade standards

Some organisations will state that they will consider ethical procurement initiatives in their sustainable procurement policy, and possibly a code of conduct. The fair trade standards aim to improve the situation of workers and/or farmers at a particular point in its supply chain.

The World Fair Trade Organisation (**www.wfto.com**) prescribes 10 principles that fair trade organisation must follow and monitor in their day-to-day work.

As with Standards or eco-labelling, there are risks in the procurement process where specifications are written by reference to a specific fair trade scheme. Where potential bidders might subscribe to any of a number of local, national or international fair trade schemes specifying one such scheme would risk claims of discrimination, potentially vitiating the process.

. . . .

CHAPTER 6

Sustainable Procurement: Drivers, Benefits and Barriers for Public and Private Sector

Why must the public sector consider sustainable procurement?

PUBLIC PROCUREMENT ACCOUNTED FOR about 19% of EU's gross domestic product[42] (GDP), and one sixth of UK GDP. The EU figure increases to 40% for spending on construction and almost a 100% for defence, civil security and emergency operations.[43] Globally, procurement is equivalent to 82% of total exports, and in OECD countries, procurement is about 20% of GDP (ICAR – http://accountabilityroundtable.org/wp-content/uploads/2014/01/ICAR-Government-Procurement-Project-Geneva-Summary-Document-Final.pdf).

The aggregation of the benefits noted by the UK of SPP and EU of GPP (http://ec.europa.eu/environment/gpp/benefits_en.htm) are that it:[44]

- allows public authorities to achieve environmental targets

- sets an example to private consumers

- raises awareness of environmental issues

- improves quality of life

- helps establish high environmental performance standards for products and services

- saves money and resources when life-cycle costs are considered

- provides incentives to industry to innovate

- can reduce prices for environmental technologies

- is an effective way to demonstrate the public sector's commitment to environmental protection and to sustainable consumption and production

- helps support innovation and economic growth

Why ought the private sector consider sustainable procurement?

A key driver for implementing a sustainable procurement policy and procedures is organisations being concerned about supply chain risks coming to fruition; whether legal, reputational or operational in nature. This extends to customers, stakeholders and staff.

Organisations that are reliant on government contracts or those SMEs looking to get involved in government projects will need to ensure that their tenders are compliant with those requirements. There are financial and other benefits to procuring sustainably.

Bidding for public sector contracts is a time-consuming process, and often an expensive one. Any private sector organisation seeking public contracts, whether directly or as part of the supply chain for a larger organisation, risks significant cost and wasted effort unless they have a full and clear understanding of the detailed requirements and policy objectives of the relevant contracting authority. Public sector agencies are taking a range of approaches to embed social value in their commissioning processes. Some have embedded social value into their procurement frameworks (such as Oldham's) or procurement strategies (such as Bath and North East Somerset's). Some contracting authorities, like Croydon have created toolkits (**www.croydon.gov.uk/contents/departments/business/ pdf/socialvalue.pdf**) for commissioners to help them build social value into procurement.[45] Others have appointed individuals with a mandate to embed social value – for instance, all major West Midlands councils have now nominated 'Social Value Champions', in partnership with Social Enterprise West Midlands, who aim to drive forward social value considerations in local authority procurement in the region. Failure to understand and to engage with those processes can easily mean wasted time and effort. Conversely, any private sector organisation, including SMEs that make the effort to engage property with social value requirements may gain access to significant volumes, and value, of business.

To take one example, highlighted in the government's review of the Public Services (Social Value) Act after its first full year of operation:

Croydon Council went out to tender for a £150 million housing repairs contract. The council used a consultation process to fully develop social value considerations. This allowed prospective suppliers to produce innovative ideas that added extra value to the service they would provide. The process produced a significant response from providers, who proposed a range of outcomes including:

- providing energy efficiency advice for residents

- initiatives that target fuel savings for customers

- DIY skills workshops for residents

- neighbourhood improvement projects

- early-stage incubation for social enterprises

- curriculum and literacy support in schools

The final contract award encompassed a number of firm social value commitments. For instance, the provider will support local employment outcomes, by providing apprenticeship opportunities, delivering careers advice in schools and offering work experience to NEETs (not in employment, education, or training) and the long-term unemployed. The contractor also delivers additional economic growth, offering mentoring and business support to SMEs in the provider's supply chain, as well as collaboration with social enterprises. Finally, the winning bidder committed to provide volunteering opportunities for staff, allowing them to contribute to local community projects.

The benefits of considering sustainability in purchasing decisions

Research, such as the PwC Report (**http://saulnierconseil.com/wp-content/uploads/2011/01/Value-of-Sustainable-Suppliers-INSEAD-Dec-2010.pdf**), has demonstrated that there are many reasons why organisations are incorporating sustainability into their purchasing decisions. Some of the benefits that have been identified are:

- reduced exposure to risk

- competitive advantage

- cost savings

- attracting and retaining talent

- anticipating legal obligations

Another key benefit of adopting a sustainable procurement strategy is the improved relationships with suppliers. Many organisations will offer advice and encourage suppliers to adopt more sustainable practices themselves and within their own supply chains.[46] The relationship between organisations and their suppliers is essential to achieving a successful sustainable procurement approach. A sustainable procurement policy can also be a means by which to engage suppliers and develop better, more strategic relationships.

Many companies also view the adoption of sustainable procurement practices as a means to gain market share and deliver better service provision. Examples of this are:

- commercial opportunities driving sustainable procurement

- improving brand value

- increasing sales with 'ethical consumers'

- meeting corporate social responsibility objectives

- avoiding negative publicity

- fostering stakeholder goodwill

In financial terms the value of the company is driven by top line growth (measurement of the speed of the company's revenue growth), its return on investment (measuring the company's effectiveness in generating income) and the weighted average cost of capital (WACC) (easing the cost of obtaining funds from financial markets).

Drawing from practice: costs vs gains

The case studies presented by the PwC report (**http://saulnierconseil.com/
wp-content/uploads/2011/01/Value-of-Sustainable-Suppliers-INSEAD-
Dec-2010.pdf**) covered a wide range of sectors, including transport,
retail, food and pharmaceuticals. Although the examples produced of
sustainability cost reduction initiatives did not take into account the
investments needed for the implementation of these actions, they present
an overall estimate of the potential financial benefits of companies
implementing a sustainable procurement initiative. The study also
presented an estimate of implementation costs for developing sustainable
procurement programmes, by looking at internal sustainable procurement
teams, third party costs for supplier audits, evaluations and follow up and
change management costs, including training, communication, process
redesign. They analysed the sustainable procurement programmes of a
typical multinational company (Global 500 company with revenue of €20
billion) and estimated the potential implementation cost of approximately
0.01% of company's revenue, representing less than 1% of the total
procurement function operating budget.

Some of the key findings demonstrating financial implications for
companies from the case study indicated:

- a correlation between sustainability related events and the
decrease in a company's share price. For example, Mattel's
share price fell by 18% in 2007 where it had to recall toys with
unacceptably high levels of lead paint. This did not include the
costs of law suits as a consequence of the incident (p. 13).

- cost reduction as a result of implementing sustainable procurement initiatives. In particular, sustainability analysis can reduce

specifications for many products (like over-packaging). For example, in 2010 DANONE France removed the outer cardboard packaging of Activia and Taillefine yoghurt saving €2.5 million (p. 12).

- reduced internal costs. For example, in 2008 Walmart, by driving fewer miles in its fleet, reduced CO_2 emissions by 200,000 metric tons. These efficiency improvements also resulted in fewer trucks on the road, less wear and tear on roads, highways and bridges, as well as savings of nearly US$200 million (p. 6).

- costs of risk reduction. For example, direct costs incurred in risk management, cost Baxter US$11 million on recall expenses of Keparin products made by a Chinese supplier in 2008 (p. 13).

- revenue growth based on companies with sustainable procurement practices. For example, Dutch retailer Ahold through its subsidiary Albert Heijn increased its sustainable trade activities and boosted revenue by 20$ million–25$ million since 2009.

A quantitative model was created by analysing the three main drivers:

- cost reduction

- risk reduction, and

- revenue growth

The model focused on their respective impact on a company's annual procurement spends, market cap and revenue. Their impact was then compared to the implementation cost of a Sustainable Procurement programme. The findings are set out below (p. 19):

Type	Description	Average results	Compared to sustainable procurement programme costs	Implementation probability
1. Cost reduction	Reduction in total cost of ownership linked to reduced energy costs, reduced consumption and reduced social and environmental compliance costs	0.05% of total revenue per project	Up to 6 times payback	High
2. Risk reduction	Financial impact on brand value from bad supplier practices (e.g. child labour, local pollution), economic cost of supply chain disruptions (noncompliance with environmental regulations)	Additional direct costs as a 0.7% of total revenue	Up to 85 times payback	Low
		Decrease of 12% in market cap	N.A.	Low
3. Revenue growth	Additional revenue through innovation of eco-friendly products/ services, price premium or income from recycling programmes	0.5% of total revenue	Up to 58 times payback	Medium

The findings indicate that that the cost reduction impact of sustainable procurement outweighs the implementation costs in almost all of the cases studied.

Common barriers to implementing sustainable procurement in both the public and private sector

Barriers are typically interrelated. Research undertaken by EPOW[47] identified the top five barriers as:

1. Lack of senior (executive) and organisational support

2. Structural and organisational change

3. Lack of coherent corporate procedures, systems and approaches

4. Lack of time resources, knowledge and capacity

5. Costs, perceived costs and cashable savings

Research on sustainable procurement challenges in the construction industry (**www.reading.ac.uk/web/FILES/tsbe/belfitt_tsbe_conf_2011. pdf**) cites the following sustainable procurement barriers, which are also true of experience in other sectors:

*   Sustainable procurement is not widely implemented even where companies adopt sustainable procurement practices. The reasons for this are listed as :

    –   'inertia' in an organisation can lead to them maintaining routine processes and failing to implement change

- staff involved feel other pressures placed on them forcing them to make decisions that do not align with a sustainable procurement strategy

- lack of motivation by staff to implement sustainable procurement strategies as a result of feeling that extra work is being given to them

The challenge for companies is how to overcome the barriers. A commitment to one of the aforementioned standards can help provide a structure to facilitate the process of embedding strategic sustainable procurement.

....

CHAPTER 7

Developing the Sustainable Procurement Strategy

THERE ARE MANY DIFFERENT DRIVERS for organisations to adopt a sustainable procurement strategy. The business case for a particular organisation will depend on a variety of issues, including the industry sector, supply chain footprint, stakeholder expectations, business strategy and organisational culture. Based on research and experience organisational culture is often not conducive to encouraging innovation in sustainability.

FIGURE 1.

SOURCE: This image has been adapted from Queensland Procurement Guidelines, October 2013: http://www.hpw.qld.gov.au/SiteCollectionDocuments/ProcurementGuideContract Disclosure.pdf

What does sustainable procurement involve?

Practical steps to developing a sustainable procurement strategy (for both public and private sector organisations):

1. Develop a sustainable procurement strategy.

   The strategy should aim to identify the key reasons for having a sustainable procurement policy. It should be centred on some clearly defined key principles or objectives to ensure that the strategy is implemented effectively. For example, a principle might be to develop tenders on the basis of whole life-cycle costs or to carry out audits of existing sustainability procurement provisions within contracts or communicating to suppliers to ensure that they procures sustainably.

2. Prepare a sustainable procurement policy

   The policy should become integral to an organisation's procurement process to drive transparency, adherence to laws, minimum standards and continuous improvement.

3. Develop a suitable labour code of conduct for suppliers

   To address business risk of unethical procurement more businesses will have established a code of conduct, setting out minimum standards of behaviour.

4. **Rethink the decision and basis of purchasing**

   For example, include factors to consider before purchasing any goods or services (such as whether there are appropriate good/services in other departments that could be put to use); prepare specifications and guidance documents to be sent to suppliers as part of tender process (ensure award criteria are included). Ask the right questions as pre-qualification stage.

5. **Include sustainability criteria into tender evaluations**

   Provided tenders will be evaluated by MEAT, sustainability criteria should be included in the tender evaluation process.

6. **Create a post-tender selection phase**

   For example, using the sustainability evaluation criteria built into the tender process (in line with EU Procurement regulations) contracts are awarded on the basis of the most economically advantageous principle.

7. **Create sustainability contract clauses (EC law permits this)**

8. **Select Key Performance Indicators reflecting the sustainability criteria set out in the tender should be included in the contract**

9. **Manage and monitor information from suppliers to ensure ongoing improvement**

What do you have in place?

The first step is understanding what procedures your organisation currently has in place to make procurement decisions, and to know who is involved in the purchasing decisions.

- has a cross-functional team been set up to develop and implement a strategy?

- has an environmental/social/profile risk assessment been completed?

- has a specific contracts risk register been compiled?

- has the organisation documented a sustainable purchasing policy?

- has this been communicated?

The planning stage is vital to developing the procurement strategy. Before developing a sustainable procurement policy, the current purchasing practices of an organisation need to be understood. The organisation must also understand its key stakeholders, legal and policy frameworks and the types of products or services purchased.

The strategy should have defined objectives and should cover risk, integration into current processes, supplier engagement, people and communications. It should also consider technologies and innovation.

For an organisation to develop a sustainable procurement strategy that will achieve measureable outcomes, it must have an understanding of those risks and opportunities that are important to the organisation in relation to its supply chain. Organisations that have not identified their sustainability issues are unlikely to have a deep understanding of their sustainability risks.[48]

Are you aware of what is 'coming up'?

Sustainable procurement is a new dimension for Chief Procurement Officers (CPOs) who until recently based their decisions primarily on price, time, and arguably quality, albeit construed narrowly. Although they may be aware of some of the questions posed below, one of the main reasons why few companies have made a strong commitment to sustainable procurement initiatives is the fact that few organisations have the necessary procedures and board-approved budget to risk implementation costs for benefits that they do not see as certain, despite the growing business case for sustainable procurement (the PwC Report). Organisational boundaries have also impacted on the problem where procurement directors are given incentives and rewards for cost reductions but not for risk reduction or contributions for revenue growth. That often falls to other people within a large organisation.

Some questions that the CPO or procurement team should consider as part of developing their strategy are, for example:

- centralised vs decentralised purchasing – what is required?

- what major products/services purchases are on the horizon?

- are there any important contracts up for renewal?

- are their long running contracts in place for certain products/ service groups?

- what of the time and financial resources available for implementation?

- what expertise is available, for example, environmental?

- outsourcing activities – what are the opportunities?

Human rights and ethical considerations are also receiving greater attention. Organisations should give consideration to where human rights issues may arise in the procurement of services or products when developing their procurement strategies. ICAR (**http://accountabilityroundtable.org/wp-content/uploads/2014/01/ICAR-Government-Procurement-Project-Geneva-Summary-Document-Final.pdf**) lists the following examples:

- contractors withholding overtime pay

- electronics that contain conflict minerals

- contractors using forced labour

- health and safety issues (giving rise to dangerous working conditions in factories)

....

CHAPTER 8

Developing a Sustainable Procurement Policy

A SUSTAINABLE PROCUREMENT POLICY should provide the foundation within which the whole procurement process operates. It should be aligned to the organisation's wider strategy or objectives. For private sector organisations that have adopted International Standards, such as ISO20121, they are required to address their supply chain and will need a sustainable procurement policy.

A good policy should:

- be specific and relevant to the procuring organisation

- address key environmental and social impacts of the goods and services being procured

- ensure legal requirements are met

- include SMART objectives, meaning targets should be specific, measurable, attainable, realistic and timely

- assign responsibility for implementation

- be effectively communicated

- include a mechanism for appropriately monitoring performance

- be endorsed by senior management

FIGURE 2.

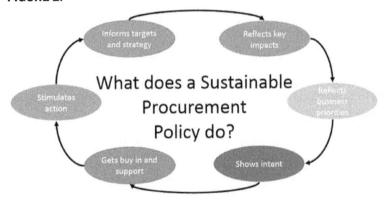

SOURCE: This image was adapted from EAUC and DEFRA.

Who should be involved?

Well-defined responsibilities and a clear understanding of the level of support needed for the project to succeed is an important consideration from the outset. An effective sustainable procurement strategy should not solely draw from the experience of the purchasing or procurement teams.

An important question to consider is therefore who will be involved, both in developing and contributing to a policy and strategy, and also driving it. This exercise will also help identify the business needs and its desired outcomes.

Breaking out from 'silos'

One of the key challenges for organisations is overcoming the 'silo' pattern of working between different functions within organisations. Challenging these silo patterns to ensure that there is cross-functional communication and co-operation. Of course, procurement officers within an organisation have a key role to play. In particular, they can:

- help shape their organisation's approach.

- work with internal colleagues (or external expertise). This should include harnessing the experience of the health and safety, legal, HR, IT and sustainability teams, as examples.

- assess the supplier market.

- feedback to colleagues about the market.

- help develop a plan for the procurement process to shape the technical, social and environmental criteria of the specification.

All too often the procurement officers are left to deal with commercial buying decisions, with little if any understanding on how to implement sustainability risk into their decisions. As mentioned above, in-house lawyers or other legally trained professionals should be included in the process. There might also be examples where the legal function fails to draw on expertise of other colleagues in developing procurement criteria.

The role of lawyers – in house and specialists

UK and European legislation on public procurement has stipulated how environmental and social considerations can be included in the public procurement process. Lawyers need to be aware of:

- how to advise their clients seeking to tender for public procurement contracts

- the thresholds applicable to a public procurement contract and the requirement to comply with statutory requirements

- how environmental and social performance requirements can be legally included within a procurement process, and

- how environmental and social performance requirements can be legally included as criteria for the award of the contract

- understand the risks of failing to comply with public procurement legislation can leave the process open to challenge, delay the process, and result in significant costs to the public body[49]

The role of the sustainability/ environmental team

The members of the environmental/sustainability team are vital for providing up to date information about the organisation's key CSR/ sustainability objectives, how the organisation is managing its ethical strategy and to provide up-to-date information about the availability of environmentally preferable goods and services. They might also be involved in communicating the strategy throughout an organisation.

It is essential to get a cross-section of people involved in developing the sustainable procurement strategy and to ensure that capacity is built within the organisation.

Working with suppliers

Engaging with suppliers is a key element of successfully implementing any sustainable procurement policy. Early engagement with suppliers of sustainable products and services is a good idea and all the policy requirements should be made clear and transparent in the tender notice or advertising procedures.

Many companies will find that working with suppliers is a journey. Providing appropriate support to help them to adapt to changing requirements in this area and that they have an opportunity to develop the capacity to meet any necessary pre-qualification requirements is good practice.[50]

It is critical to establish open and honest relationships between key purchasing staff and suppliers. New sustainability requirements can affect suppliers as it may require them to change their processes and possibly products.

Developing relationships with suppliers is also important for organisations seeking to protect their financial, operational and reputational risk. The impact of suppliers on an organisation's brand value is increasingly problematic in an era where products and services come from 'emerging markets' or low labour cost locations.[51]

A comprehensive understanding of the relationship with suppliers is essential. Some of the key considerations include:

- which suppliers pose the greatest risk to the environment (with associated implications for regulatory, financial and reputation risks);

- whether some suppliers may be unfairly disadvantaged by the initiatives, for example, smaller suppliers;

- who can provide the greatest efficiency and cost savings or have the capacity to source and supply cost-effective sustainable products;

- what are the best means to engage and communicate effectively with suppliers.

SOURCE: http://www.eauc.org.uk/tools_resources

Engagement with suppliers

Ongoing engagement and communication with suppliers and stake-holders is key. Organisations should consider mapping their suppliers. There are various tools available to organisations to help develop their approach (for example: BS903). An active analysis of an organisation's stakeholders will enable organisations to ensure the proactive influencing and managing of people or groups that can impact or will be affected by the organisation's sustainable procurement initiatives. In addition to mapping an organisation's stakeholders, organisations should also prioritise those suppliers that are critical to the organisation and those that pose the greatest risk.

Once organisations have identified their key stakeholders, they should consider the best method of communicating with them, including the most effective media to use. Developing the communication responsibilities of the team should also include understanding the expertise and experience of team members and their existing relationships with stakeholders.

BS8903 highlights the following as important principles for effective stakeholder engagement:

- the desired objectives associated with the engagement

- the appropriate scope of sustainability requirements across the supply chain, stakeholder groups and/or organisations

- what the key messages actually are and who the target audience is

- how those messages are relevant to the stakeholders

What about training and guidance?

In a research paper[52] conducted by Walker and Philips a common theme that emerged is the requirement within the purchasing and supply profession for education. This applies across the private and the public sector so that they can learn to incorporate sustainable and ethical criteria in their buying decisions. There is a need to share best practice across both sectors. On a practical level, to successfully implement a sustainable procurement strategy, staff must have appropriate practical skills, knowledge and access to information.

Training may be needed on:

- how to integrate sustainability considerations into the tender procedures

- where to find assistance to develop sustainability criteria

- how to assess and verify sustainability claims made by the tenderers

- how to evaluate life-cycle costs in tendering

CHAPTER 9

The Procurement Process

What are the key issues to consider in the procurement process?

IN BOTH PUBLIC SECTOR and private sector procurement, sustainability principles can be incorporated into the whole procurement process:

- defining the need
- evaluating options
- design and specification
- supplier selection
- tender evaluation
- post-contract management

The ISO20121 guidance also refers to including supplier development into the process.

Understanding the distinction between the selection and award stages

The sustainable procurement legislation for the public sector makes a clear distinction between the selection and the award stages.

In the selection stage, criteria can be set to relate to the contractor and include aspects such as economic and financial standing as well as professional and technical knowledge.

In the award stage offers are examined and the best one chosen, based on which supplier offers the best price or the most economically advantageous tender. Current EU legislation and case law emphasise a strict distinction between the two stages.

If the private sector is going to adopt best practice principles to embed sustainable procurement in their purchasing decisions, they should adopt these differentiations.

Including sustainability criteria in tender evaluations

There are two main ways in which tenders can be evaluated:

- the lowest price

- MEAT (most economically advantageous tender)

In order to achieve sustainability in procurement, tenders should be evaluated according to MEAT.

The EU procurement directives require that the award criteria should be set out either in the contract notice or in the tender documents.

Case law has helped establish the level of detail required for the advertisement of award criteria.

The notice or contract should indicate:

- whether the contract will be awarded on the basis of the lowest price only or MEAT

- the criteria and sub-criteria that will be applied (if using MEAT)

- the weighting which you will apply to each criteria in the evaluation[53]

Award criteria for public procurement contracts must be linked to the subject matter of the contract.

It is not strictly necessary to explicitly use the term 'sustainability' or 'sustainable' in the subject matter of the contract. However, it is advisable to include them to make it very clear that the contract aims to serve those broader social and environmental objectives as well as more directly functional objectives.

To explain the point, **Clientearth.org** distinguishes between 'horizontal' and 'functional' objectives. For example, the procurement of cleaning services or paper clips would each serve a functional objective. However, a contracting authority may choose to promote broader policy objectives – for example, taking into account reduction of CO_2 emissions. The Court of Justice of the European Union (CJEU) 2002 *Concordia Bus* case[54] held that under the procurement directives at the time a contracting authority organising a tender procedure for the operation of bus services could include among the award criteria under MEAT, criteria to take into account the nitrogen oxide emissions and noise level of the bus fleet offered by parties in the tender.

Award criteria are not selection criteria

There is often confusion about the selection and award stages. Award criteria must not examine issues that should be addressed at selection stage or which have already been addressed at selection stage, such as, the financial capacity of tenderers.

Pre-qualification questionnaires

A prequalification questionnaire is usually made available to potential suppliers. A scoring system is usually included explaining how tender submissions will be scored to ensure that a fair weighting is given to suppliers providing more sustainable solutions. For example, a score of '0' is given to an incoherent response that is limited to the minimum regulatory requirements of social, economic and environmental issues. Contrastingly, a score of '10' will be given to a well-structured response showing a good understanding of social and environmental policies, and the ability to innovate.

....

CHAPTER 10

Practical Considerations During Selection and Award Stages

Checklist for sustainability risk assessment

PUBLIC PURCHASERS HAVE AN OBLIGATION to get the best value for money and to be fair in procurement procedures. Value for money can include environmental and social criteria. Being fair means providing equal opportunities and guaranteeing transparency. Best practice requires private sector procurement professionals to consider the same.

Procurement will start with the planning stage: understanding the organisation's needs. For example, there are particular sectors from which an organisation may procure goods or services where human rights violations are common. A key question is whether those rights are covered in the procurement decision-making process (ICAR – **http://accountabilityroundtable.org/wp-content/uploads/2013/11/ ICAR-Government-Procurement-Project-Geneva-Summary-Document- Final.pdf**).

A sustainable procurement risk assessment can be used to identify the different sustainability risk associated with purchasing a specific service or product.

There are a number of steps that an organisation should follow in creating its strategy but also as part of the decision to procure.

These steps are summarised below:

1. The first question that an organisation should address is whether there is a need to purchase the good or service or if the need can be met another way? (See Appendix A for an example of a 'demand analysis'.) Challenge the decision to procure! (CLASP info – **www.claspinfo.org/ resources/simple-steps-environmentally-sustainable-procurement- -putting-policy-practice-final**).

2. Determine if there are obvious business risks in the contract. For example, is the contract essential to deliver the organisation's vision? Would recovery costs be high if the purchase failed? Are there a limited number of suppliers? (EAUC – **www.eauc.org.uk/ tools_resources**).

3. Create a sustainability impact assessment – this will assist in determining the specific sustainability issues, risks and opportunities that the procurement of the goods/services will address and support. For example:

IMPACT	ISSUES
Energy	• energy use and efficiency
	• use of renewable energy, e.g. solar

Information gathered during stakeholder consultations can also be used to establish sustainability objectives.[55]

4. Consideration of all sustainability issues (not only environmental issues) should be included in the sustainability risk assessment.

Examples of sustainability risk are:

a. Causing harm to the environment.

b. Risk to the organisation's reputation (human rights abuses or failure to secure key natural resources.

c. Breaches of law/costs of fines or penalties.

d. Risk of missing opportunities to aggregate benefits across service delivery.

5. Next rate the risk depending on its frequency or severity. For an example of a sustainability impact scoring chart:[56]

CRITERIA/QUESTION	RATING/SCORE
Does the procurement have a significant environmental or social impact/risk?	3. High – significant environmental or social impact/risk
	2. Medium – some environmental or social impact/risk
	1. Low – little or no environmental or social impact/risk
What degree of influence does the public authority/ organisation have in the particular supply market?	3. High – high level of influence
	2. Medium – moderate level of influence
	1. Low – minimal influence
Does the procurement align with or support the public authority/organisation's strategic and sustainable business goals?	3. High – strong alignment
	2. Medium – moderate alignment
	1. Low – little or no alignment

6. Use the risk scoring to determine the procurement action that will be taken in the specification. For example, where a sustainability risk is high, but the contract is of low value it may be a priority to seek more sustainable options and include sustainability specifications for contract award. Where the risks may be low but the contract is of high value, the procuring organisation may seek to raise awareness with their suppliers of their related policies and focus on the higher risks to manage during the course of the contract.

Forum for the Future (**www.forumforthefuture.org/projects/buying-a-better-world**) has produced guidance on how to map procurement areas against the level of impact.

Specification writing and pre-commercial procurement

A good specification is fundamental. It should, where appropriate, incorporate sustainability requirements in as much detail as possible.

The European Union's procurement laws and procedures have developed from the Supply and Works Directives of the 1960s and 1970s, which had as their main objectives open advertising of contracting opportunities, prohibition of discriminatory specifications and the use of objective criteria for tendering and award procedures.

Through successive revisions EU procurement has moved away from a process based primarily on price to a far more complex analysis of 'most economically advantageous tenders' (MEAT), allowing contracting authorities to include broader environmental and social factors when producing a procurement specification and when evaluating bids.

Emerging models of best practice are characterised by:

1. Early market engagement, allowing the contracting authority to identify the range of technologies that are either currently available or in development.

2. 'Outcome specification' describing the result sought rather than prescribing the technology to be purchased.

3. Detailed and weighted evaluation criteria, designed to allow radically different technologies and solutions to be meaningfully compared against the desired outcomes.

Those elements of best practice have been identified through projects such as Smart SPP. The project was funded by the European Commission and conducted by a consortium led by ICLEI (Local Governments for Sustainability). The Smart Sustainable Public Procurement project focused on Europe, where public authorities spend approximately €1.5 trillion a year on goods and services (equivalent to 16% EU GDP). ICLEI's case is that:

From constructing energy efficient public buildings to buying low emission vehicles, from buying organic or Fair Trade food to installing water-saving toilets, public procurement can have a huge impact in driving the market towards sustainability.

These elements are set out in more detail below and can be used by both the public and the private sector in developing best practice principles.

. . . .

CHAPTER 11

Smart SPP

AT THE CORE of Smart SPP is the identification of a contracting authority's needs in terms of performance and function. The first step is for the contracting authority to decide upon and articulate the result it seeks, for example, a percentage reduction in greenhouse gas emissions or in energy costs. The next critical step is communicating that requirement to the market in a way that allows bidders to suggest the best, most efficient way to achieve the stipulated result.

Inevitably, this approach is likely to elicit widely differing proposals, some involving the purchase of goods, others of services. In one example, a contracting authority's desire to reduce energy costs could have been met either by purchasing new voltage optimisation equipment, or by contracting for management and consultancy services to secure the more efficient use and operation of existing building management systems.

A major advantage of the Smart SPP approach is that it is not constrained by the existing technical knowledge or market awareness of the contracting authorities' officers responsible for the procurement process. Identifying and communicating the desired outcome leaves it to bidders to introduce technologies and solutions that the contracting authorities would have had no other viable way of finding.

A major challenge any contracting authority is to devise and implement evaluation and award criteria that allow comparison of the full range of proposed solutions. That creates a significant training requirement and a need for both proactive advice and a robust methodology to insulate the process from legal challenge. Smart SPP provides some examples of weighted criteria for various product lines, but demonstrated a pressing need for increased skill levels among procurement officers, and for the sharing of best practice within and between contracting authorities.

Early market engagement

Early market engagement is a key element of Smart SPP. Providing a sufficiently long lead-in time allows potential bidders to consider what potential alternative solutions exist, or are close to market readiness. It may allow potential bidders to reallocate time and resource to accelerate the development and commercialisation of particular products or innovations to meet a contracting authority's requirements.

To maximise the efficiency and effect of this process, it is vital for contacting authorities to engage not just with their regular suppliers, including university knowledge-transfer functions and SMEs. True innovation may be found in start-ups and small enterprise, and not just in the slick research operations of large corporations.

This stage of 'pre-commercial procurement' has the additional advantage of allowing contracting authorities to demonstrate a commitment to identifying potential suppliers from outside existing and established supplier relationships. Firmly pegged to objective criteria, that approach promotes transparency, economic inclusion and demonstrably fair process.

Life-cycle costing

Smart SPP focuses attention of the life-cycle cost and benefits of the technology to be purchased. The initial purchase price is no real guide to the whole-life benefits of a particular solution. The costs of operation (particularly energy and water consumption) must also be taken into account, along with the costs of maintenance and final decommissioning and disposal. A bid that 'wins' in terms of coming in with the lowest initial price may, over the full life-cycle, compare poorly to others that have a higher initial price. Within the EU, increasingly strict waste regulation means that end of life costs are rapidly emerging as a key, and sometimes determinative, criterion.

Non-financial criteria

Smart SPP urges contracting authorities to allocate significant weighting to non-financial criteria, such as improved energy efficiency ratings or measurable and verifiable greenhouse gas reductions.

SME-friendly tenders

As well as early market engagement to identify, and potentially accelerate, innovation, Smart SPP recommends that contracting authorities should consider splitting tenders into lots in order to make the volume both manageable and worthwhile for SME bidders.

Where lot sizes cannot sensibly be reduced, contracting authorities may consider either public–private partnership models to facilitate volume (e.g. by contributing to the expansion of manufacturing facilities) or allocating significant weight to criteria promoting joint ventures between large corporations and SMEs.

Risk allocation

Smart SPP recognises that contracting authorities tend to be risk-averse, and that buying innovation inevitably entails a degree of risk, whether technical or financial. This element requires extremely careful management and legal protection.

Clear and accurate identification of the areas of risk allows for their contractual allocation between the parties. As well as considering the appropriate lot sizes for a tender, contracting authorities should consider whether a piloting phase might be included to allow for the testing at scale of the chosen technology or range of technologies.

Monitoring performance

Introducing an innovative solution cannot end with the signing of the contract. Monitoring performance and impact allows lessons to be learned and applied for future procurements, and may prompt improvements to or adaptation of the chosen technology to meet circumstances that were not originally taken into account (e.g. opportunities arising from the convergence of energy efficiency and electronic communications in window technologies). As with the other elements of Smart SPP, this places additional responsibilities on contracting authorities, and may require a step-change in the levels of training, advice and expertise required by those authorities to deliver an effective procurement regime.

Writing specifications

From the perspective of a procurement or contract management professional the use of procurement procedures to advance broad policy objectives has led to greater complexity and risk. Where a process involved inviting bids for specifically defined works, goods or services the principal objective was to secure delivery at the lowest price. Where innovation is invited, or broader social or economic benefits are to be secured, there is inevitably far greater scope for uncertainty and, therefore, for challenge.

Specification has usually been the first step in the procurement cycle. Before potential bidders can be identified, and before any meaningful invitations can be issued the contracting authority must identify and clearly articulate the works, goods or services it wishes to obtain.

There has been a significant move away from specifications that describe in detail the items to be procured and towards 'outcome' or 'performance' specifications. Outcome specifications give potential suppliers the opportunity to respond flexibly and innovatively, using their experience and knowledge of technologies and solutions that may otherwise be extremely difficult to identify.

Outcome specifications explained

Outcome or performance specification describes the function of the product or service. It is based on describing the result to be achieved, not on dictating the way in which it is to be reached. It contrasts with a more prescriptive approach that sets out the characteristics of a solution that is within the knowledge or experience of the person or team writing the specification.

Outcome specification tends to produce more concise and apparently simpler specifications. However, their practical effect from a contracting authority's perspective is to shift complexity from initial specification to the design and operation of evaluation and award criteria. Where the specified result may be achieved through a variety of means or approaches, the contracting authority must design a process that allows meaningful comparison of bids that may have radically different characteristics. Those solutions may range from significant capital projects to energy audit, training and consultancy services. The following case study illustrates the point.

Procurement of energy solutions for local authority housing and education

The overall brief is to achieve measurable reductions in 1) energy costs, 2) greenhouse gas emissions and 3) energy efficiency ratings. A key challenge for CCPO is to achieve those results across a mixed portfolio of properties. Participating contracting authorities are also keen to promote local employment and business opportunities and to demonstrate strong sustainability credentials. To that end, CCPO has been instructed so far as possible to consider how far the overall project can be broken down into lot sizes likely to attract bids from small- and medium-sized enterprises within the areas served by the contracting authorities. There is also a strong policy directive from the contracting authorities to ensure that the process promotes the development of innovative technologies and techniques.

The contracting authority or organisation wishes to reduce its energy consumption and greenhouse gas emissions and to improve the energy efficiency ratings of premises within its portfolio. It may receive bids from technology companies offering energy efficient plant and equipment, from others offering voltage optimisation technology and from others offering consultancy services promising to achieve the specified results by making better use of equipment that is already in place.

However, it is clear from the brief that stakeholders in the process have other, broader, policy objectives. They include the promotion of local employment and business opportunities.

Faced with diverse objectives, it is essential for the contracting authority to design evaluation and award criteria that can, so far as possible, be reconciled when comparing bids. For example, the policy directive of promoting the development of innovative technologies and techniques might be reconciled with the objective of attracting SME bids and of promoting local business opportunities if the contracting authority is able to identify potential bidders through avenues such as Knowledge Transfer Partnerships offered by universities to promote the commercialisation of research and innovation.

There would be a strong case for early engagement with potential suppliers or pre-commercial procurement. Crucially, those involved in the process of writing and developing specifications may have little or no knowledge or awareness of technological developments, particularly any at an early stage of development or commercialisation. For a case study describing a highly effective approach to this issue see developed by Procura+ and the Eastern Shires Purchasing Organisation, see:

http://www.sustainable-procurement.org/fileadmin/template/
scripts/sp_resources/_tools/put_file.php?uid=131f7a5f

A crucial part of this process also requires those within a contracting authority responsible for producing specifications to gather information and detailed requirements from the full range of internal stakeholders. Those stakeholders will certainly include the department or team that will either itself be the end-user or will be responsible for delivering to end-users the relevant works, goods or services. However, where broader policy objectives are to be pursued it is highly likely that other departments or teams will have input. In those circumstances, a key task for the procurement professional must be to question and challenge those inputs where they consider that they would result in conflicting specifications or that they would militate against achieving the core objectives of the current procurement process. There is a material risk that loading procurement processes with too many policy objectives militates against the basic task of securing either the lowest price or the most economically advantageous outcome from the tender. Trying to achieve too much can lead to achieving too little.

Both the case study and the template below can be used in public and private sector procurement.

A useful template for specifications might include the following headings:

Purpose of specification	What is the aim of this scope of services? Express this in (at most) 2–3 sentences.
Roles	What will be the respective roles of the supplier (when appointed) and of the contracting authority? These will clearly differ if the proposed contract is for the one-off delivery of goods or to form the basis for an ongoing commercial relationship (e.g. delivery, installation and ongoing maintenance of plant and equipment).
Key aspects of performance	How will good or satisfactory performance be recognised? This is a key element of contract management. Express this in (at most) 2–3 sentences.
Key personnel	For consultancy or other professional services or for the provision of innovative or technological solutions it is likely that certain roles will be necessary to secure delivery. Clearly, at the point of specification it is possible only to refer to those roles in functional terms. It will be for bidders to propose individuals or teams to fulfil those roles as part of their bids, and the appropriateness of those individuals or teams (e.g. in terms of qualifications) may be taken into account when evaluating those bids.
Detailed specification	This may be expressed either in terms of the key tasks to be performed, as details of units of service/volume or as details of the services to be provided OR in outcome terms, perhaps prefaced with 'The provision of the [Services] will result in the following outcomes.'
Contract management	This section may be used to set out details of the proposed format and frequency of contract management reviews, including any Key Performance Indicators (KPIs) that will be applied. Inclusion of this element is a useful reminder that procurement is not about awarding a contract; it is about securing full and proper performance of that contract.

CHAPTER 12

Practical Considerations and Examples of the Pre-Qualification Questionnaire, Tender Specification and Weighting Criteria

Pre-qualification questions with examples

THE PREQUALIFICATION QUESTIONNAIRE (PQQ) is used to assess if a business fulfils a set of criteria that complies with the fundamental needs and expectations of a tendering authority or organisation. An organisation must be compliant before it can proceed to the next stage, i.e. the invitation to tender).[57] There is limited scope to address sustainability at this stage; however, organisations can include prequalification criteria that demonstrate:

- no prosecutions for environmental or health and safety breaches in a given period

- how suppliers can support the organisation's sustainability strategies

Examples of pre-qualification questions

Two examples of pre-qualification questions are set out below. These apply to both the public sector and to the private sector adopting best practice principles.

1. Delivery of catering services

An example of what an organisation may include at this stage in relation to sustainability criteria could be:

The contract award will be based on the Most Economically Advantageous Tender (MEAT). Although value for money is a crucial factor in determining the outcome of the tender process, evaluating the most economically advantageous bid will take into consideration the following criteria before a final decision is made:

- operational risk

- environmental considerations

- level of organic produce used

- contractual risk, terms and conditions

- costs[58]

2. Supplier's operations

Environmental management

Does the supplier have a programme or system in place to identify environmental impacts relevant to the organisation or a programme/ system under development with a timeline for implementation?[59]

Practical examples for tender evaluation criteria

Where an organisation is seeking to achieve sustainability in procurement, tenders should be evaluated by MEAT. This applies to the private sector organisations adopting best practice principles.

There are different approaches that can be taken for supply categories. The tender response should be evaluated in accordance with a pre-agreed scoring methodology.

Examples of questions for suppliers and checklists for evaluation:

Examples of questions	Examples of criteria
Systems for environmental management: Describe the system, processes and practices that enable your organisation to meet your legal environmental requirements and achieve continual improvement of your environmental performance	Criteria to be commented on in response to this question Existence of an operational Environmental management system (EMS) Organisations sustainability/ environmental policy
Employment practices: What does your organisation do to apply fair employment practices to your workforce employees and sub-contractors?	Check organisation's documented policy for workforce and labour practices, for example reference to the UN Global Compact, or the UN Guiding Principles for Business and Human Rights

The UK Environment Agency has identified 10 products/services with the greatest environmental and social impact.[60] These are:

1. aggregates

2. chemicals

3. construction

4. energy

5. horticulture

6. machinery (including pumps)

7. IT/electronics

8. timber

9. vehicles/plant

10. waste management

What about weighting?

The procurement team or officer must decide how they will assess the level of commitment and performance of a supplier in relation to environmental and social sustainability.

Officers must select criteria or questions most appropriate for their procurement requirements.

The following are examples of how tender submissions can be scored to ensure fair weighting is given to those suppliers providing sustainable solutions.

Qualitative assessments

It is not recommended that qualitative assessments are made for product specific criteria. It may be appropriate where suppliers are asked to detail their sustainability performance. Suppliers will be asked to identify their main social and environmental impacts associated with their business and identify adequate measures to manage these impacts to achieve a higher score.[61]

Example of a weighting scorecard that can be used

Mark	Tender scoring guidance
10 – Excellent	Clearly structured response showing an understanding of social, economic and environmental priorities, good ability and sympathy with sustainable procurement and good ability to innovate.
7.5 – Good	Well structured response showing an understanding of social, economic and environmental priorities, good ability and sympathy with sustainable procurement, some ability to innovate.
5 – Satisfactory	Relatively unstructured response that is receptive to social, economic and environmental priorities, some ability, experience and sympathy with sustainable procurement, little interest in innovating.
2 – Poor	Unstructured response which is limited only to the regulatory requirements of social, economic and environmental priorities, little ability or sympathy with sustainable procurement, little ability to think innovatively.

0 – Unsatisfactory   Incoherent response which is limited only to the minimum regulatory requirements of social, economic and environmental priorities, very little ability and no sympathy with sustainable procurement, no ability to think innovatively.

SOURCES: MOD sustainable procurement commercial policy statement: **http://media. claspinfo.org/sites/default/files/Enviro_Sustain_Procurement_FINAL.pdf** and adopted from London Centre of Excellence Sustainable Procurement Project and CLASP.

Documenting evaluation of tenders

It is recommended that evaluation documentation is produced. This document should:

- summarise the weighting criteria

- the indicators used

- the scores awarded to each tender

- confirmation that the relevant environmental/social threshold has been reached

- the weighted score

- the total 'environment/social score for each tender (the environment agency suggests this is the total score for that tender divided by the maximum score achieved by any tender)

CHAPTER 13

Practical Considerations for Contract Management

Defining the subject matter of a contract

THE 'SUBJECT' MATTER OF A CONTRACT is about what product, service or work you want to procure. The procurement laws do not in terms restrict the subject matter of a contract. The principles of sustainable procurement are more concerned with how the products/services are procured, not with the precise identity or nature of those products or services. There are some safeguards built into EU legislation – these are thresholds, above which certain rules apply and the requirement that technical specifications must not be defined in a certain way.

Key Performance Indicators (KPIs)

Ensuring that the right KPIs are inserted in the contract is another challenge for organisations. All too often the tender requirements do not match the requirements in the contract, or are simply not accounted for.

Research conducted by Walker and Philips[62] confirm that there is also a 'confusing array of indicators pertaining to sustainable procurement'.[63]

They set out some examples of how the challenge of indicators can be overcome with a suggestion that an organisation only focuses on five.

This approach should not necessarily be followed, as the number of indicators will depend on the key sustainability risks identified for each project/service. However, they do make useful suggestions on how to overcome some of the sustainability risks.

For example, where waste is identified as a risk, the challenges will be disposal costs, landfill having a finite availability, and outsourcing of services. Their suggestion is that indicators that can be used to overcome these challenges are:

- waste reduction targets

- recycling targets

- increase use of waste as a fuel

- include waste reduction targets criteria in outsourced contracts

Indicators should be:

- simple and readily understandable

- easy to assess against

- related to the delivery of environmental benefits/social benefits or reduction of environmental costs

Examples of KPIs to include in contracts:

- *Catering provisions*

  - The contractor shall, unless otherwise agreed in writing between the parties:

    - use recycled materials in the provision of packaging

- use packaging that is capable of recovery for further use or recycling

- ensure all packaging complies with applicable EU and UK legislation

- *Improved performance*

The supplier shall, within three months of the date of this Agreement, submit a Sustainable Procurement Plan to the Council's representative for approval, which approval shall not be unreasonably withheld.[64]

The limits of contract management systems

Contract management software has become widely available in recent years and provides an excellent means of controlling costs and minimising the risk of missing deadlines. Typically, contract management software allows the organisation to:

- upload and organise contract documents

- link related contracts

- set alerts for renewal/extension deadlines

- identify responsible individuals

- set escalation/reporting milestones or events

- compare data across contracts (e.g. price, costs)

- incorporate notes about suppliers

- set out details of dispute escalation/resolution procedures

- track variations, including price reviews.

However, contract management software cannot adequately address all issues relating to the lifecycle of a contract. For example, contract variation might arise not from an express amendment but from conduct amounting to waiver or setting up an estoppel preventing a party from insisting on compliance with a particular obligation. Relevant conduct can include an oral representation made by an employee.[65]

The law remains unclear as to the possibility of oral variation where a contract includes a clause stating that variation must be in writing.[66]

Crucially, even the most sophisticated contract management system cannot interpret contracts or determine the outcome of any enforcement action. Consequently, it remains necessary for experienced contract managers and advisors to keep contracts under active review and to be alert to the implications of judicial decisions. In the following section, we highlight some key issues for contract review.

....

CHAPTER 14

Key Issues to Consider When Reviewing Contracts

IT IS ESSENTIAL TO MONITOR the performance throughout the life of the supply arrangement. Sustainability can be monitored alongside quality, delivery, service and price. The most effective means of providing a framework to monitor sustainability performance indicators (KPIs) and/ or reporting requirements is to ensure that the KPIs are measurable and clearly defined and that sustainability is included as an agenda topic in regular meetings with suppliers.

When a contract has ended, sustainability performance should be included as part of the overall contract review process. The information should assist in identifying areas for improvement and form the basis of whether the contract should be renewed or extended.

In order for organisations to effectively measure and monitor the results of sustainable procurement, they must measure the baseline position.

Reviewing contracts: Key contract terms

The principal objective of procurement is to obtain for the contracting authority the delivery of agreed works, good or services. The proposed form of contract is generally provided as an element of the invitation to tender. Consequently, procurement professionals must be familiar with key elements of contract law to assess whether the proposed form sufficiently protects the interests of the contracting authority.

Key contract terms include:

- warranties

- time limits and deadlines

- liquidated damages and indemnities

- termination provisions, whether for breach of triggered by events or circumstances beyond the parties' reasonable control or contemplation

Warranties

In English contract law warranties and representations have different legal bases and effects. A warranty is a statement of fact made as part of a contract. If the statement of fact proves to be false then there is a breach of contract, and the remedies are contractual. A representation is also a statement of fact, but it is one made before the contract is created. If a representation has induced a party to enter into a contract, and it proves to be false, then the remedy lies in tort.

The difference is significant. If a false statement of fact can be shown to have been a pre-contract representation then the innocent party may elect to rescind (end) the contract and seek an order the effect of which is to put that party as far as possible back in the position it would have been in had the contract not been made. Crucially, if a false statement can be shown to have been a misrepresentation, then it might be open to the innocent party to seek tortious damages that may be considerably higher than those available under the contract. This point was graphically illustrated in *BskyB v EDS*.[67] BskyB entered into a contract for the provision of a subscriber management system. The contractor's managing director was subsequently found to have made a number of statements about the contractor's technical capacity and ability to deliver on time. Those statements proved to be false, and to have been made fraudulently.

The finding of fraudulent misrepresentation was highly significant. Liability for fraudulent misrepresentation cannot be excluded. The contract value was approximately £48 million. There was a contractual liability cap of £30 million. BskyB's initial claim was in excess of £700 million. The matter eventually settled at a reported £318 million.

The facts of BskyB were unusual, and the finding of fraudulent misrepresentations seems to have been greatly influenced by a barrister's success in demonstrating that the managing director had lied about his qualifications. The barrister obtained the equivalent MBA online for his pet dog Lulu. Lulu's certificate indicated that she had obtained higher marks than the managing director. Having undermined his credibility on that point, the barrister was able to cast doubt on all other aspects of his evidence.

The court's more usual approach is to lean against any finding that a remedy in tort is available and that the innocent party can bypass a contractual limit on liability. That more common approach was evident in *Sycamore Bidco v Breslin*[68] where the judge rejected the claim that an error in accounts could be treated either as a contractual warranty or as a tortious misrepresentation. Mann J found that even where a contract clause uses the phrase 'warrants and represents' it is likely that the statements of fact to which the clause relates would be regarded only as a contractual warranty. That reasoning is consistent with the Court of Appeal ruling in *Bottin v Venson Group*.[69] In Bottin the court considered the use of very clear words stating that:

> *the Warrantors acknowledge that the Investor is entering into this Agreement in reliance upon the Warranties and agree that the Investor may treat them as representations inducing them to enter into this Agreement.*

Although apparently extremely clear, the court considered that it would make 'no commercial sense' to allow a claim for misrepresentation where the effect would be to bypass a contractually agreed cap on liabilities.

In practice, a party entering into a contract in reliance on a particular statement of fact wishes to make it clear that an action should be available in tort then the wording probably needs to be even clearer than that in *Bottin*. In addition to an acknowledgement and agreement that statements may be regarded as representations and that the innocent party was induced by those statements to enter into the contract, it is probably necessary to state that the remedies for breach in the event that those statements prove false should be through an action for misrepresentation and that remedies could include rescission and damages for misrepresentation.

Where questions of sustainability and sustainable development are concerned, it may be that the information provided to confirm the supplier's environmental and sustainability credentials would be sufficiently important to justify wording designed to make it clear that liability would not be subject to the agreed contractual cap.

It is also necessary to consider the specific importance of each warranty. For example, where a contracting authority decides to purchase innovative or cutting-edge technology to achieve the outcomes described in its specification, it is necessary to ensure that all elements of the technology can be used without risk of challenge. Increasingly, innovative technology is being developed and then commercialised by means of joint ventures between university knowledge transfer teams, start-up or early stage businesses that are spinning out of research departments and either public or (more commonly) private sector investors. Ensuring that all relevant intellectual property rights will be transferred or licensed to the contracting authority may well determine whether the technology can be used. A specific warranty to that effect would certainly be required, and it may be a point of such importance as to fall outside any general contractual cap on liability.

Liquidated damages

Liquidated damages can provide an extremely useful and straightforward remedy for breaches such as late delivery. However, the principal risk when providing for liquidated damages in a contract governed by the laws of England and Wales is that the sums may be considered too high, and liable to striking down as a 'penalty'. If found to be a penalty, the specified sums are not recoverable. They are considered to have been set as a level designed to deter a breach by providing for a remedy that is disproportionate to any actual loss or damage that might be suffered.

Recently, the court has taken a more flexible line when assessing whether sums specified as liquidated damages are, in fact, a penalty. In determining whether a sum could legitimately be regarded as liquidated damages, the court would previously ask only whether it represented a 'genuine pre-estimate' of loss or damage. Where a sum reflected a genuine pre-estimate then it would be recoverable even if it exceeded actual loss. In *Azimut-Benetti v Healey*[70] the court adopted the 'commercial justification test' from the Court of Appeal ruling in *Murray v Leisurplay*,[71] finding that 'a clause may be commercially justifiable provided that its dominant purpose is not to deter the other party from breach'. The judge found that where a clause has a 'clear commercial and compensatory justification' for both parties, it was not a penalty and was, therefore, enforceable. The judge noted generally that where both parties are legally represented and the contract had been freely entered into, the court should uphold the terms the parties have agreed to, where possible.

In practice, although the 'commercial justification' test is more flexible than the previous 'genuine pre-estimate of loss' test, it remains the safer course to set liquidated damages at a level that can be justified by reference to a clear, objective and genuine pre-estimate. However, in all cases where a contract is to provide for liquidated damages it is strongly advisable for the parties to:

record, in writing, reasonable justification for any amount specified in a liquidated damages clause, in particular explaining why it is a genuine pre-estimate of loss; consider whether an alternative provision may be available, and retain records of all negotiations.

Alternative performance?

In some circumstances it may be possible to avoid the question of whether sums provided for in a contract would be at risk of being struck down as a penalty. The approach would be to set out in a contract alternative methods: for performance of contractual obligations, with a different price attached to each. For example, a clause might state:

The Supplier must deliver the Goods by 1 December 2014. If the Supplier does not deliver the Goods by 1 December then the Supplier must pay by way of liquidated damages the sum of £1000 for each day's delay until actual delivery of the Goods.

Faced with that clause, the court would have to consider whether a daily sum of £1,000 could be regarded as either a genuine pre-estimate of loss or damage stemming from non-delivery of the Goods, or whether there was any other commercial justification for damages being set at that level. The risk would remain that the daily sum would be struck down as a penalty.

An alternative approach might be to provide:

The Supplier must deliver the Goods to the Contracting Authority.

If the Supplier delivers the Goods on or before 1 December 2014 then the Price will be £100,000.

If the Supplier elects to deliver the Goods at any time after 1 December then the Price will reduce by £1000 each day.

In the second clause the Supplier is not obliged to deliver the Goods by 1 December. The Supplier has an express choice between different ways to perform the basic obligation to deliver the Goods. If the Goods are not delivered by 1 December, there is no breach and therefore no basis for striking down the daily Price reduction as a penalty.

The concept of alternative performance found some support in *Berg v Blackburn Rovers*.[72] A football manager had been appointed on a contract providing for a fixed term of five years. The manager was dismissed after only 57 days. The football club initially admitted liability to pay the full balance of the salary for the fixed five-year term, but then applied to withdraw that admission. The football club argued that the clause providing for payment of the full five-year salary ought to be struck down as a penalty.

The court disagreed. The football club had negotiated a right to dismiss the manager early and without notice. The price for that right was the football club's agreement to pay the balance of the manager's salary should the right be exercised. There was no breach. The court referred to Lord Roskill's observation in *Export Credits Guarantee Department v Universal Oil Products Company*:[73]

> *The clause was not a penalty clause because it provided for payment of money upon the happening of a specified event other than a breach of contractual duty by the contemplated payer to the contemplated payee . . .*
>
> *. . . the main purpose of the law relating to penalty clauses is to prevent a plaintiff recovering a sum in respect of a breach of contract committed by a defendant who bears little or no relationship to the loss actually suffered by the plaintiff as a result of the breach by the defendant. But it is not and never has been for the courts to relieve a party from the consequences of what may in the event prove to be an onerous or possibly even a commercially imprudent bargain.*

While 'alternative performance' clauses offer the possibility of avoiding any argument that a sum specified as the financial consequence of a particular decision is a penalty, they must be used with care. In many cases, it would not be viable to offer the supplier a choice of methods or timings for performance of an obligation. For example, where the delivery date for goods or services from one supplier formed part of a larger project, lead-in times and other coordination factors might make a particular method or date for performance crucial. In those cases, it remains necessary to check that sums payable on breach can be justified either as a genuine pre-estimate of loss or on broader commercial grounds.

Termination

The principal objective of procurement is to obtain for the contracting authority the delivery of agreed works, good or services. Where the contract is for the one-off delivery of goods or a single service, termination provisions may be of little importance, as the contract comes to an end once that transaction has completed. However, where a contract provides for an on-going relationship it is vital to ensure that contracting authority has the ability to bring the relationship to an end should any serious difficulties arise.

Common termination events include:

- breach or non-performance

- supplier insolvency or criminal conviction

- external circumstances, such as changes in law or regulation

Terminating events must be spelled out in very clear language to avoid claims that the contract has been wrongfully brought to an end. It is also necessary to consider whether termination of a contract ought to bring all liabilities to an end, or whether it is necessary to provide for the survival of any terms of the contract. For example, if the contract included confidentiality obligations or obligations to use technology or information only for the purposes of the specified project, then those obligations would probably have to continue to bind the parties.

How will termination clauses be influenced by the 2014 Directive?

Termination issues are likely to become more regularly significant, and clauses more rigorously negotiated, under the new suite of procurement Directives adopted in April 2014. They include provisions designed to encourage the formation of 'innovation partnerships' between contracting authorities and private sector companies, particularly SMEs.

Innovation partnerships are required to contract by reference to the stages of development of new technology or solutions. The principal justification for innovation partnerships is that they offer a way for public sector funding to incubate and provide a scalable market for cutting-edge and research-based products and services. Public sector investment is designed to be an early-stage boost.

Any public sector investment in private sector enterprise must avoid falling foul of EU rules on state aid. Consequently, innovation partnership contracts must allow for termination at the end of each stage of development, allowing the public sector body to withdraw once the innovation that is, in effect, being 'sponsored' has gained sufficient traction to survive on a purely commercial basis.

Termination of innovation partnerships will involve some extremely difficult issues concerning the ownership and rights to use and exploit inventions or innovations stemming from the relationship. Where public sector funding has been used to incubate innovation, it is only right that the public sector body ought to have a share in the value generated by that process. However, it does not follow that the public sector body either should, or could. Take anything like full ownership of innovations. In practice, the more likely outcome is an agreement to licence any innovations on terms that allow the public sector body to use and to incorporate them into its own services. Those provisions would have to be contractually capable of surviving termination of the initial innovation partnership.

It is also necessary to check the procedures for termination of any contract. Where termination is to be effected by notice, consider whether the notice provisions would work in practice. Particularly difficult issues can arise in practice where notice provisions are couched in generic terms and allow (for example) service of notice by email or other electronic means. Unless it is clear that email addresses or other messaging services will be properly and regularly monitored, service of crucial notices by electronic means can lead to extensive – and expensive – disputes over validity. Termination is an event of such commercial and legal significance that there is a strong case for including separate and specific notice provisions to ensure that the process works smoothly and efficiently.

....

Conclusions

THE GROWTH IN LEGISLATION covering procurement and supply chains is increasing. There is also a more acute awareness by business with global supply chains that the operational, financial and reputational risk of sourcing their products and services needs to be properly managed through their purchasing decisions. Both the public and the private sector are going to have to revisit how they procure their services and products. There is a growing need to train procurement professionals to understand the social and environmental aspects that can impact on their tenders and contracts. There also appears to be a trend for organisations to share their procurement practices more broadly. Increased transparency in reporting and advertising will contribute to this trend. However, there is still a lot of work to be done to engage those organisations that have not or are not willing to embrace the organisational shifts that will need to be made. Only then will sustainable procurement practices become more mainstream and better integrated into business decision-making processes.

Appendix[74]

FIGURE 3. Demand analysis: Questions to consider.

1. Do we really need to purchase this good or service, or can the need be met in another way?

   - is a suitable good/service already available within the organisation?

   - can existing assets be refurbished, repaired or upgraded to meet the need?

   - are there other options for meeting this need, e.g. reuse, borrow and swap?

   - can the need be met in partnership with another organisation?

   - what would avoid the need for this good/service?

2. Can we reduce the quantity or scale of the goods or service whilst achieving the same service delivery?

   - how do the goods or services contribute to service delivery? Are we automatically replacing based on past procurement patterns?

   - are specifications based on actual requirements, ensuring that they are not over-specified?

   - are improved technology options available?

- are there options for behaviour change in relation to consumption of this good or service?

3. Can alternative goods or service be used to meet this need?

   - is there another more sustainable good or service available that can serve the same purpose? Have there been any technology improvements?
   - could a service be used to meet the need instead of a good (e.g. purchasing cloud hosting instead of a server)?

4. Can the goods/service be specified to have improved sustainability outcomes, including being able to serve a useful purpose after its initial use?

   - can the goods or its key components be reused, refurbished, repaired, recycled and composted?
   - what specifications could be included to reduce the use of resources (such as energy, water or consumables) during the useful life of the goods?

5. What information is available regarding sustainably-preferable options for this purchasing requirement? Where can more information be obtained about suitable alternatives?

   - is there an environmental officer/sustainable procurement expert within the organisation?
   - what information is provided by suppliers?
   - what external sources of information are available, e.g. other government bodies, trade organisations, NGOs, research institutes?

References

FOR **FURTHER INFORMATION** on the material touched on in this book refer to following links:

Legislation

EU

EU Public Procurement Directives http://ec.europa.eu/environment/ gpp/eu_public_directives_en.htm

EC Procurement Thresholds http://www.ojec.com/Threshholds.aspx

Explanatory Memorandum to the Public Contracts Regulations 2006, 2006 No. 5 http://www.legislation.gov.uk/uksi/2006/5/pdfs/ uksiem_20060005_en.pdf

The 2014 Procurement Directives:

- Public Sector http://eur-lex.europa.eu/legal-content/EN/TXT/ ?uri=OJ:JOL_2014_094_R_0065_01

- Concessions http://eur-lex.europa.eu/legal-content/EN/TXT/ ?uri=OJ:JOL_2014_094_R_0001_01

- Utilities http://eur-lex.europa.eu/legal-content/EN/TXT/ ?uri=OJ:JOL_2014_094_R_0243_01

UK

HM Government. The Public Services (Social Value) Act 2012: One year on. https://www.gov.uk/government/uploads/system/uploads/attachment_data/file/275719/Public_Services__Social_Value__Act_-_One_Year_On.pdf

Procurement Reform (Scotland) Act 2014 http://www.legislation.gov.uk/asp/2014/12/contents/enacted

Transposing the 2014 EU Procurement Directives https://www.gov.uk/transposing-eu-procurement-directives

EU and UK Government guidance and policy

EU

Communication on the Sustainable Consumption and Production and Sustainable Industrial Policy Action Plan http://ec.europa.eu/environment/eussd/pdf/com_2008_397.pdf

Buying Green! A Handbook on Environmental Public Procurement http://ec.europa.eu/environment/gpp/pdf/buying_green_handbook_en.pdf

Life-Cycle Costing http://ec.europa.eu/environment/gpp/lcc.htm

UK

Sustainable Development in Government. Sustainable Procurement. http://sd.defra.gov.uk/advice/public/

Sustainable Procurement: http://sd.defra.gov.uk/advice/public/

EU Public Procurement http://ec.europa.eu/trade/policy/accessing-markets/public-procurement/

Defra. Greening Government Commitments: Operations and Procurement. http://sd.defra.gov.uk/documents/Greening-Government-commitments-Jul2011.pdf

Defra. Sustainable procurement in Government: Guidance to the Flexible Framework. http://sd.defra.gov.uk/documents/flexible-framework-guidance.pdf

National Sustainable Public Procurement Programme http://sd.defra.gov.uk/advice/public/nsppp/

Defra. An Action Plan for Driving Sustainable Operations and Procurement across Government. http://archive.defra.gov.uk/sustainable/government/documents/ap-driving-sustain-ops.pdf

Standards, tendering guidance, tools and best practice

BS8903:2010 http://shop.bsigroup.com/en/ProductDetail/?pid=000000000030203003&rdt=wmt

ISO20121 http://www.iso.org/iso/home/standards/management-standards/iso20121.htm

World Fair Trade Organization http://www.wfto.com/

Government Buying Standards http://sd.defra.gov.uk/advice/public/buying/standards/

Government Buying Products http://sd.defra.gov.uk/advice/public/buying/

REFERENCES

Central Point of Expertise on Timber **https://www.gov.uk/government/ groups/central-point-of-expertise-on-timber**

Example of EU Green Public Procurement Sheet (Copying and Graphic Paper) **http://ec.europa.eu/environment/gpp/pdf/toolkit/paper_ GPP_product_sheet.pdf**

Procurement at the Environment Agency **https://www.gov.uk/ government/organisations/environment-agency/about/procurement**

South West Food and Drink. Supplying food into the public sector: Tendering guidance. **http://www.southwestfoodanddrink.com/ uploads/publicprocurement/supplying_food_into_the_public_sector_ tendering%20_guidance.pdf**

Forum for the Future. Buying a Better World. **http://www.forumfor thefuture.org/project/buying-better-world-sustainable-procurement- toolkit/overview**

Greening Government Commitments: Guidance on Measurement and Reporting **https://www.gov.uk/government/uploads/system/ uploads/attachment_data/file/61172/Greening_20Government_ 20Commitments_20-_20guidance_20on_20measurement_20and_ 20reporting.pdf**

Inspiring and creating social value in Croydon **http://www.croydon.gov. uk/contents/departments/business/pdf/socialvalue.pdf**

UN Global Compact and Business for Social Responsibility. Supply Chain Sustainability: A Practical Guidance for Continuous Improvement. **http://supply-chain.unglobalcompact.org/site/article/68**

Procurement

Tate, Wendy, 2013. *The Definitive Guide to Supply Management and Procurement*. London: CMSP.

Public Procurement and Innovation http://ec.europa.eu/enterprise/policies/innovation/policy/public-procurement/index_en.htm

Sustainable business

Theron, C. and MacKenzie, S. 2012. CLT envirolaw: Setting standards for sustainable business. *ELM* 24(6).

Theron, Colleen, 2011. Sustained risk. *Business Law Review*, April.

Sustainable procurement: Definition, emerging issues and implementation, barriers and challenges and benefits and drivers

http://saulnierconseil.com/wp-content/uploads/2011/01/Value-of-Sustainable-Suppliers-INSEAD-Dec-2010.pdf; http://saulnierconseil.com/wp-content/uploads/2011/01/Value-of-Sustainable-Suppliers-INSEAD-Dec-2010.pdf

Queensland Government Chief Procurement Office. Sustainable Procurement a Working Definition. http://www.hpw.qld.gov.au/SiteCollectionDocuments/SustainableProcurementDefinition.pdf

Government of Western Australia. Sustainable Procurement Practice Guidelines. http://www.finance.wa.gov.au/cms/uploadedFiles/Government_Procurement/Guidelines_and_templates/goods_and_services_sustainable_procurement_practice_guidelines.pdf?n=4084

REFERENCES

Benefits of GPP http://ec.europa.eu/environment/gpp/benefits_en.htm

Belfit, Sexton and Schweber, Handcock. Sustainable procurement: Challenges in the construction industry. http://www.reading.ac.uk/web/FILES/tsbe/belfitt_tsbe_conf_2011.pdf

Walker, H. and Philips, W. 2009. Sustainable procurement: Emerging issues. *Int. J. Procurement Management* (Vol. 2, No. 1).

CLASP. Simple steps to environmentally sustainable procurement – Putting policy into practice. http://media.claspinfo.org/sites/default/files/Enviro_Sustain_Procurement_FINAL.pdf

Smart SPP http://www.smart-spp.eu/

Client Earth. Briefing No. 4: Clarifying the link to the subject matter for sustainable procurement criteria. http://www.clientearth.org/reports/procurement-briefing-no-4-clarifying-link-to-the-subject-matter.pdf

European pathway to zero waste. Implementing sustainable procurement: overcoming common barriers. http://www.wrap.org.uk/sites/files/wrap/Implementing%20sustainable%20procurement%20-%20summary%20v2.pdf

EAUC on Making the Business Case http://www.eauc.org.uk/tools_resources

Queensland Government. Procurement guidance: Integrating sustainability into the procurement process. http://www.hpw.qld.gov.au/SiteCollectionDocuments/ProcurementGuideIntegratingSustainability.pdf

Ethical procurement and human rights

CIPS, 2013. Ethical and sustainable procurement. http://www.cips.org/
Documents/About%20CIPS/CIPS_Ethics_Guide_WEB.pdf

Stumberg, Ramasastry, Atreya, 2013. Government procurement:
Promoting procurement policies that ensure business respect for
human rights. Summary of forthcoming report, December. http://
accountabilityroundtable.org/wp-content/uploads/2013/11/ICAR-
Government-Procurement-Project-Geneva-Summary-Document-Final.pdf

Qatar Foundation Mandatory Standards of Migrant Workers' Welfare
for Contractors and Sub-Contractors http://www.qf.org.qa/app/
media/2379

Stop the Traffik http://www.stopthetraffik.org/

Finance against Trafficking http://www.financeagainsttrafficking.org/

Notes

1. http://ec.europa.eu/trade/policy/accessing-markets/public-procurement/

2. http://sd.defra.gov.uk/advice/public

3. Communication (COM (2008) 400).

4. http://saulnierconseil.com/wp-content/uploads/2011/01/Value-of-Sustainable-Suppliers-INSEAD-Dec-2010.pdf

5. BS8903 is a British Standard developed to help organisations and individuals consider and implement sustainable practices within their procurement processes.

6. http://www.cips.org/Documents/About%20CIPS/CIPS_Ethics_Guide_WEB.pdf

7. See Stumberg et al., 'Government Procurement: Promoting Procurement Policies that Ensure Business Respect for Human Rights'.

8. For more discussion on this case, see Titcombe and Theron, Applying the UN Guiding Principles in the fight against Human Trafficking' at **www.finance againsttrafficking.com/resources**

9. See ChainChecker, a tool to help companies identify if they are inadvertently supporting human trafficking in their organisation and supply chain: **www. financeagainsttrafficking.com**

10. Also enact the provisions of existing Council Directive 89/665/EEC, on remedies for public sector procurement, transposed on 31 January 2006, the deadline for transposition by the EU.

11. Utilities regs 2006 in a similar way implemented 2004/17/EC: Coordinating the procurement procedures of entities operating in the water, energy, transport and postal services sectors.

NOTES

12. http://ec.europa.eu/environment/gpp/eu_public_directives_en.htm

13. http://www.legislation.gov.uk/uksi/2006/5/pdfs/uksiem_20060005_
en.pdf Explanatory Memorandum to the Public Contracts Regulations 2006
2006 No. 5

14. http://ec.europa.eu/environment/gpp/eu_public_directives_en.htm

15. 2004/18/EC

16. See Regulations 6, 7 and 8 for more exclusions.

17. Generally means a written contract for the purchase or hire of goods by a
contracting authority (Regulation 2).

18. A written contract for the carrying out of a work or works for a contracting
authority, or where a contracting authority engages a person to procure a
contract for works to specified requirements (Regulation 2).

19. These are listed in Schedule 3 of the Regulations.

20. Regulation 8(1).

21. See for a list of the latest thresholds.

22. http://www.legislation.gov.uk/asp/2014/12/contents/enacted

23. *BskyB v EDS* [2010] EWHC 86 (TCC).

24. Tate, 2013. The definitive guide to supply management and procurement, p. 79.

25. http://ec.europa.eu/environment/gpp/lcc.htm

26. (COM (2008) 400) and accompanying Staff Working Document (July 2008).

27. (COM (2001) 274).

28. (COM (2009) 215 final).

29. For an example: http://ec.europa.eu/environment/gpp/pdf/toolkit/paper_
GPP_product_sheet.pdf

STRATEGIC SUSTAINABLE PROCUREMENT: AN OVERVIEW OF
LAW AND BEST PRACTICE FOR THE PUBLIC AND PRIVATE SECTORS

30. An Association representing local government interests within the UN and at other international policy forums. Founded in 1990 as the International Council for Local Environmental Initiative; now called Local Governments for Sustainability http://www.iclei-europe.org/

31. Buying Green, p. 4.

32. http://archive.defra.gov.uk/sustainable/government/documents/ap-driving-sustain-ops.pdf

33. http://sd.defra.gov.uk/documents/Greening-Government-commitments-Jul2011.pdf

34. Theron and MacKenzie, 2012, CLT envirolaw 'Setting Standards for Sustainable Business'.

35. http://sd.defra.gov.uk/advice/public/buying/standards/

36. http://sd.defra.gov.uk/advice/public/buying/products/

37. www.defra.gov.uk/documents/spec-wood-products.pdf

38. http://shop.bsigroup.com/ProductDetail/?pid=000000000030203003

39. http://www.southwestfoodanddrink.com/uploads/publicprocurement/supplying_food_into_the_public_sector_tendering%20_guidance.pdf

40. See guidance on inclusion of Fairtrade products in a specification: http://www.dfpni.gov.uk/index/procurement-2/cpd/cpd-policy-and-legislation/content_-_cpd_-_policy_-_procurement_guidance_notes/content_-_cpd_procurement_guidance_notes_pgn_02_-_06/df1_10_13781_v2___pgn_02_06_procurement_of_fair_trade_products__dec_2010_.pdf

41. See LexisPSL Environment for further information

42. http://ec.europa.eu/enterprise/policies/innovation/policy/public-procurement/index_en.htm

43. http://ec.europa.eu/enterprise/policies/innovation/policy/public-procurement/index_en.htm

NOTES

44. http://ec.europa.eu/environment/gpp/benefits_en.htm

45. http://www.croydon.gov.uk/contents/departments/business/pdf/socialvalue.pdf

46. https://www.gov.uk/government/organisations/environment-agency/about/procurement

47. European Pathway to Zero Waste, 'Implementing sustainable procurement: overcoming common barriers', 2010/2011.

48. Theron, Colleen, 2011, 'Sustained risk', p. 55.

49. See LexisPSL Environment and In-house Advisor for further information

50. CLASP, 'Simple Steps to Environmentally Sustainable Procurement: Putting Policy into Practice.

51. Tate, Wendy, 2013, 'The definitive guide to supply management and procurement', pp. 30–31.

52. Walker and Phillips, 2009, 'Sustainable procurement: emerging issues', p. 41.

53. See GPP, p. 39 for examples of case law interpretation on criteria.

54. Case C-513/99 *Concorida Bus Finaland Oy Ab v Helsingin Kaypunki and Hkl-Bussiliikenne* [2002] ECR1-7123.

55. http://www.finance.wa.gov.au/cms/uploadedFiles/Government_Procurement/Guidelines_and_templates/goods_and_services_sustainable_procurement_practice_guidelines.pdf?n=4084

56. p. 12, http://www.finance.wa.gov.au/cms/uploadedFiles/Government_Procurement/Guidelines_and_templates/goods_and_services_sustainable_procurement_practice_guidelines.pdf?n=4084

57. http://www.southwestfoodanddrink.com/uploads/publicprocurement/supplying_food_into_the_public_sector_tendering%20_guidance.pdf

58. Adapted from http://archive.defra.gov.uk/foodfarm/policy/publicsectorfood/

toolkit/documents/index.htm. Always get legal advice on these issues.

59. See LexisPSL Environment for further information.

60. The Environment Agency Sustainable procurement guide.

61. p. 24, http://www.hpw.qld.gov.au/SiteCollectionDocuments/ProcurementGuide IntegratingSustainability.pdf

62. Walker and Philips, 2009, 'Sustainable procurement: emerging issues'.

63. Ibid., p. 50.

64. CLASP, 'Simple Steps to Environmentally Sustainable Procurement- Putting Policy into Practice'.

65. See, for example, the Australian case *GEC Marconi v BHP Information Technology* (2003) 201 ALR 55; or in England and Wales *Morris v Baron* [1918] AC 1, HL.

66. *Globe Motors v TRW Lucasvarity Electric Steering* [2012] EWHC 3134 (QB); *I-Way v World Online Telecom* [2002] All ER (D) 114 (Mar).

67. [2010] EWHC 86 (TCC).

68. [2012] EWHC 3443 (Ch).

69. [2004] EWCA Civ 1368.

70. [2010] EWHC.

71. [2005] EWCA Civ 963.

72. [2013] EWHC 1070 (Ch).

73. [1983] 1 WLR 391.

74. Queensland Procurement Guide.

For Product Safety Concerns and Information please contact our EU
representative GPSR@taylorandfrancis.com
Taylor & Francis Verlag GmbH, Kaufingerstraße 24, 80331 München, Germany

www.ingramcontent.com/pod-product-compliance
Ingram Content Group UK Ltd.
Pitfield, Milton Keynes, MK11 3LW, UK
UKHW040928180425
457613UK00011B/309